T0308086

The Jewish Holidays

Precursor to Redemption

by

Rabbi Yosef Gabay

Penina Press

The Jewish Holidays: Precursor to Redemption

Text Copyright © 2011 Yosef Gabay

Cover Design: Shanie Cooper
Typesetting and production: Daniella Barak
Editor: Batsheva Pomerantz

All rights reserved. No part of this book may be used or reproduced or transmitted in any form or by any means, electronic or mechanical, including photocopying, recording, or by any information storage and retrieval system, without written permission from the publisher.

Hard Cover ISBN: 978-1-934440-42-1
First edition. Printed in Israel.

Distributed by:

Urim Publications
POB 52287
Jerusalem 91521, Israel
Tel: 02.679.7633
Fax: 02.679.7634
urim_pub@netvision.net.il

Lambda Publishers, Inc.
527 Empire Blvd.
Brooklyn, NY 11225, USA
Tel: 718.972.5449
Fax: 781.972.6307
mh@ejudaica.com

www.UrimPublications.com

בס"ד

Rabbi Zev Leff

הרב זאב לף

Rabbi of Moshav Matityahu
Rosh HaYeshiva—Yeshiva Gedola Matityahu

מרא דאתרא מושב מתתיהו
ראש הישיבה—ישיבה גדולה מתתיהו

D.N. Modiin 71917 | Tel: 08-976-1138 טל' | Fax: 08-976-5326 פקס' | ד.נ. מודיעין 71917

Dear Friends,

I have read portions of the manuscript "Israel's Redemption Through the Holidays" by Rabbi Yosef Gabay. As the author writes in his introduction "These celebrations (the holidays) were given to Israel to enhance our connection with G-d, to study His Torah, to refine our character traits and to reflect upon our life's mission." The author presents essays that reveal the various aspects of the holidays that help enable us to understand their deeper message and thus utilize them to fulfill their true purpose.

As in his previous works Rabbi Gabay presents us with many and varied Torah sources that he weaves into a beautiful tapestry to present the message of the various holidays in depth and breadth.

I found the portions that I read to be informative, interesting, and inspiring, and assume that the remainder of the presentation follows suit.

May Hashem grant Rabbi Gabay life and health and the wherewithal to continue to merit the community from his wellsprings of Torah knowledge.

Sincerely,
With Torah blessings
Zev Leff
Rabbi Zev Leff

ב"ה | בית מדרש גבוה | בית מדרשו של רבנו הגאון רבי אהרן קוטלר זצוק"ל
Beth Medrash Govoha / Rabbi Aaron Kotler Institute for Advanced Learning
617 SIXTH STREET / LAKEWOOD, NEW JERSEY 08701

בס"ד

הנה רצה לחזק ידי הרה"ר יוסף פנחס גבאי שליט"א, מחשובי תלמידי חכמים
בעיר לוס אנגלס, אשר מידי ביקורי שם נפגשתי אתו ונהניתי לקבל ספרו
החשוב, ובתוכו רבות מאמרים בענייני יסודי אמונתנו הטהורה והשקפת תורתנו
הקדושה, מיוסדים על פי רבותינו הגדולים ז"ל, ערוכים ומבוררים בשפה המדוברת,
ובקש ממני שאכתוב דברי הסכמה. והנה מלבד שאדוני לא הגעתי לידי
ידיעה נכונה ביסודות אלו, גם לא הספקתי לעבור כל הספר לעיין היטב,
אמנם מהנקודות שראיתי נהניתי מאד, ונראה שיש בזה תועלת
לאלו לדעת אחרי הטהורים והקדושים, וגם נראה שהכל [illegible]
בספרי קודש [illegible]
על נעימה לבקש להגביר שעות אלו לתורה ולעבודה,
ויהי שיזכה להוציא לאור עולם ולהמשיך דרכו ועבודתו בקודש
מתוך מנוחה והרחבת הדעת עד כי יבא שילה בב"א,
הכותב לכבוד התורה ומוקיריה
דוד ב"ר [illegible] שוסטאל
כ"א אדר תשס"ט ליקוואוד יצ"ו.

Rabbi Gabay has presented the fundamentals of Jewish Faith and Torah Hashkafa in a clear and engaging manner. Undoubtedly, many will benefit from the content of this book as it will strengthen their spiritual quest. I commend the author for his work. May Hashem grant him full success in reaching out and inspiring Am Yisrael.

Rabbi Dovid Schustal
Beth Medrash Govoha
Lakewood
Adar 21, 5769

Contents

INTRODUCTION

The holiness of Shabbat and the Jewish holidays represent a moment of serenity in stormy seas. These celebrations were given to us, the Jewish People (Am Yisrael), to enhance our connection with God, to study His Torah, to refine our character traits and to reflect upon our life's mission. That is why we humbly praise God for His kindness: "*Ata bechartanu mikol ha'amim...*" – "You chose us from among all the nations; You loved us, and You favored us; and You exalted us above all peoples; and You sanctified us with Your commandments; and you drew us near, our King, to Your service; and Your great and holy Name did You proclaim upon us."

If one plants a vibrant rose in the beach sands, it will wither within hours no matter how many times he will water it. The nature of the ground is simply not conducive to its growth. It will not flourish because the soil nutrients are missing. But, if the flower is planted in a healthy environment, it will surely blossom. Likewise, despite our exile, Shabbat and the holidays represent the fertile soil for the spiritual growth of the Jewish individual.

When the disciples of Rabbi Elazar asked what one should do to spare himself the pangs of the Messianic era, he answered that one should study Torah and practice kindness toward others.[1] It is so because during the Messianic times, there will be a different World Order. It will no longer be governed by greed, prestige seekers, egoism, irrelevant passions and arrogance. Instead, the new society will pursue Torah, selfless kindness, and a quest for spiritual growth. As there is little doubt that we

1 BT *Sanhedrin* 98b

are standing at the door post of this worrisome and exalted period, and considering the brazen falsehood which shamelessly confronts us every moment and everywhere, it only makes sense to adopt the advice of the wise Rabbi Elazar.

Judaism's fundamental tenet is enclosed in the words of the Mishna: "This world is like a lobby before *Olam Habbah*, the World to Come. Prepare yourself in the lobby so you may enter the banquet hall."[2] From the Torah point of view, any worldly activity which does not lend itself to this objective is to no avail. A Jew's material and spiritual pursuits must, at the end of the day, lead to the successful fruition of this tenet. Judaism's *hashkafa*, outlook, stands in stark opposition to the commonly expressed idea that "we only live once, let's have fun." In *Olam Habbah*, the concept of limitation and time are unknown; instead, it is identified with eternity. Am Yisrael earns access to *Olam Habbah* thanks to Shabbat observance, as one carries into his weekly activities the holiness of Shabbat.

The good, the retributions and struggles, along with the exiles and their persecutions, are all part of the hallway that leads to the fulfillment of God's plan for the Jewish individual and people. It is a world so sublime that even the ministering angels, the Seraphim and Ofanim, cannot inherit.

The true significance of man is defined by his personal motivation, otherwise known as the good or evil inclination.[3] Man's heart can lean toward noble traits or malevolent behavior. This is the true meaning of "*zeh le'umat zeh assah Elokim*" – that God has created, within each individual, opposing forces of comparable influence to counter each other. The greatness of an individual reveals an equal amount of evil which he subdued through personal effort. Likewise, man's specific character weakness is a clear indication of his potential for greatness. If one is led by his desires to satisfy certain immoral pursuits, he should know that within himself, there is as much goodness to reverse his negative cravings.

Although this world may look disappointing, in reality there is no evil that comes from God. Yet, there is a disturbing paradox which many

2 *Avot* 4:21

3 R. Tzaddok HaKohen of Lublin, *Tzidkat Tzaddik* 248

struggle to comprehend. As the Sages tell us that God's intent in creating the world consists in bestowing His goodness upon all creatures, where do we find the realization of this goal?[4] On the contrary, we seem to be constantly surrounded by evil. The wars, the diseases, malnutrition and torture are rampant. So are social injustice, poverty and a persistent glorification of falsehood. Where then is the unhindered flow of divine kindness upon the world? We must conclude that God's infinite bounty cannot be dispensed in our finite and material world. We live in the lobby, the hallway that leads to the World to Come where material restraints are absent. On the tortuous journey of this world, we ready ourselves to partake of God's endless bounty.

The struggle continues from generation to generation until the advent of Mashiach when God's Name will be glorified throughout the world. It is so because the deliberate defiance of Godliness diminishes God's glory in the world. It becomes Israel's role to defeat destructive ideologies and elevate God's Name around the world, to promote the concept of divine justice and to remind mankind that this world is not ownerless.

Toward the end of each lunar month, the moon's brightness fades away until it disappears, when it aligns itself with the sun. While a period of darkness settles in, we remain aware that it is only temporary. Within a few days and without doubt, the moon will reappear in its full splendor. This infallible characteristic of the moon equally identifies the destiny of the Jewish People. The latter's life cycle experiences moments of darkness and tragedies, knowing that it is momentary. Like the moon, Am Yisrael is convinced of upcoming brighter days and looks with a seasoned eye at the scorn of other nations. Notwithstanding all their turbulent history and suffering, in time, Israel will experience a renewal and be a light unto the nations. This message is paramount to Jewish belief. Faith in God represents a fundamental tenet of Judaism. The pain of the Jewish People is not accidental. Its long years of suffering and national humility are the results of God's *hashgacha pratit*, divine involvement, in small and large events. Thus Israel's greatness is manifest in its fall as much as it is in its rise. In the midst of their darkness, the Jews are focused on the upcoming

4 R. Moshe Chaim Luzzato, *Mesilat Yesharim*, Introduction

ray of light which will shine, as surely as the moon's surface will lighten up in the new month. In sum, Israel's confidence in God remains unaltered in their darkest moments as much as during their glory.

This book attempts to inform the reader on the significance of the Jewish Holidays' celebration as well as on their spiritual effects on the world. When the People of Israel celebrate a Jewish holiday, it is not merely to commemorate a recurring historical event. Rather, it is to perform a specific *tikkun*, a spiritual betterment to the cosmic world at large, and to the well being of the Jewish People. It is so, because the Divine Light which descended onto the world the first time the event occurred flows again on its anniversary every year.[5] Every Pesach, we experience the same Divine Light which unleashed the energy to redeem the enslaved Israelites from Egypt. Likewise, at the Giving of the Torah, a Divine Light of a different holiness and nature descended upon Mount Sinai, enabling the Israelites to witness several miracles. Similarly, a unique Divine Light permeated the Land of Israel enabling the Hasmoneans' victory over the Greeks. The same supernatural energy descends to the world on Rosh Hashana, Yom Kippur, Sukkot and Purim. As the Divine Light returns to earth during the observance of each holiday, its spiritual benefits to the world are optimized when the Jews consume the matzah, blow the *shofar*, dwell in the Sukkah, read the Megillah, or light the Chanukah lights.

During the days of the Beit Hamikdash, the Temple, the Divine Light was always present in Jerusalem. Its presence translates into blessings, abundance, peace and harmony. On the other hand, divine concealment is manifest through epidemics, social upheavals and wars. The resurgence of the Divine Light on earth, and the *tikkun* performed through the religious observance of the holidays will bring Israel's redemption closer. ■

5 R. Moshe Chaim Luzzato, *Derech Hashem*, 4:8

Pesach

Pesach

There are times when prayer is to no avail as the prosecuting forces in heaven are just too overwhelming. When the Israelites stood by the Red Sea, they were not deserving of any miracles.

In heaven, the prosecuting angels argued before God against Israel: "The Egyptians worshipped idols and the Israelites worshipped the same idols!" They rightly claimed: "So why should You, Hashem, save these and drown the others?"

On account of this irrefutable argument, we often find passages in the Talmud describing the splitting of the Red Sea as a "difficult decision." Indeed, it was a hard choice for God. His propensity to give and act with kindness is restrained by our shameless deeds. The prosecuting voices are strong and it is difficult to weaken their case. Hence, God tells Moses: "Why do you cry out to Me?" This is not the right time for prayer as it will not help. Rather, the only act that will justify your salvation is: "Speak to the Children of Israel and let them journey forth!" Tell them to show their full bitachon, *reliance on Me, by stepping into the raging waves. In fact, the merit of reliance on God overrules any heavenly prosecution, regardless of the latter's strength of arguments. Notwithstanding man's sins, the trait of* bitachon *in God triggers heavenly compassion to flow upon the world.*

THE SHECHINAH IS WITH US IN EXILE

Imparting the tale of the Exodus is an imperative, as through the story we keep our children informed of God's miracles and kindness.[1] It is a Torah commandment to read the Haggadah on the night of Passover. At one point during the recitation, we raise our individual wine cup and sing: "*Vehi she'amdah la'avoteinu,*" – "It is this that has stood by our fathers and us." Indeed, it is the promise that God had made to Abraham that stood by us in all generations, through countless persecutions.

However, on a deeper level, *vehi she'amdah* refers not to that promise. Rather, it invokes the Divine Presence which is also in exile with us.[2] The survivability of the Jewish People in the hostile lands of the Diaspora is directly credited to the *Shechinah*'s presence and protection.

Rabbi Shimon bar Yochai teaches: "As a sign of God's love for Am Yisrael, He sends His *Shechinah* into exile with them. Later on, when they will return to the Holy Land, the *Shechinah* will also accompany them."[3] In support of his teaching, Rabbi Shimon quotes God's promise to end Israel's exile: "'Then, Hashem, your God, will bring back your captivity and have mercy upon you.' [4] While the correct grammatical form should read: '*veheshiv*' – 'He will bring back,' it reads instead: '*veshav*' – 'He will return.' It is to indicate that God will return with them from all their exiles."

First, let us try to understand what the *Shechinah* represents. In *Tehillim*, King David refers to it as *Em Habanim*, the mother of the children.[5] The concept of *Shechinah* refers to a Divine Light which encompasses all the root *neshamot*, souls, of Israel. It is so called because it dwells (*shochen*) down on earth. It is also called *Knesset Yisrael*, as it gathers in (*koness*) all the souls of Am Yisrael. As this Divine Light is comprised of Israel's *neshamot* in a state of remarkable unity, then *Em Habanim*, the

---

1 Exodus 13:8 "And you shall tell your son on that day, saying, 'it is because of this that Hashem acted on my behalf when I left Egypt.'"

2 R. Pinchas Friedman, *Shvilei Pinchas*, Jerusalem, Pesach 5768

3 BT *Meggilah* 29a

4 Deuteronomy 30:3

5 Psalms 113:9 "He transforms a barren wife into a glad mother of children. Halleluyah!"

mother of the children rejoices. However, in times of exile, the *Shechinah* is in distress on account of her children's suffering.[6]

The *Shechinah*'s spiritual power is all dependent on Israel's deeds. When they observe the Torah, then God releases a flow of kindness upon the *Shechinah*. But when they abandon the Torah's way of life, then the *Shechinah* becomes the recipient of austere judgments. In the first case, blessings and abundance flow upon Am Yisrael; in the second situation, Israel is pushed into exile. However, the *Shechinah* too goes into exile to watch over Am Yisrael and to make sure that they will never totally assimilate with the nations. Its presence also guarantees our eventual redemption as God will ultimately bring back the *Shechinah* to dwell in Jerusalem: "They shall make a Sanctuary for Me – so that I may dwell among them."[7] The concept of *galut haShechinah,* the exile of the *Shechinah*, is likewise addressed by the Prophet: "and for your rebellious sins that your *mother* [the *Shechinah*] has been sent away."[8]

In fact, this remarkable concept of the exile of the *Shechinah* is first addressed when Yaakov Avinu journeyed to Egypt with his seventy offspring. Then, God appeared to him and reassured him with these words: "I shall descend with you to Egypt, and I shall surely bring you up."[9] Through Jacob, Israel's first exile had begun. It was the start of God's decree which was conveyed earlier on to Abraham: "And He said to Avram, 'Know with certainty that your offspring shall be aliens in a land not their own, and they will serve them, and they will oppress them, for four hundred years.'"[10]

Now we can explain why we raise the cup of wine when we recite *vehi she'amdah. Knesset Yisrael* – that is, the *Shechinah* which gathers in the souls of Am Yisrael – is likened to a cup of wine over which a blessing is uttered.[11] Just as the cup is but a recipient of whatever is poured inside, so the *Shechinah* can only receive what God releases onto it. We raise the

6 The Arizal, *Shaar Hakavanot, Drushei Halayla* 4
7 Exodus 25:8
8 Isaiah 50:1
9 Genesis 46:4
10 Ibid., 15:13
11 Zohar, Vayechi 250a

cup of wine to highlight the presence of the *Shechinah* with us in exile and to underline the fact that in every generation, hostile kingdoms rise against us to annihilate us, but the Holy One, Blessed is He, rescues us from their hand.

Likewise, when God first appeared to Moses, He did so over a bush, a diminutive and humble setting, rather than a tall and imposing tree. It was to convey to Moses that the Divine Presence, the *Shechinah*, is also in exile, to share the pain of the Jewish People.[12] This is the idea of "*immo anokhi be'tzarah*" – "the *Shechinah* shares Am Yisrael's grief."

Moses was confused when he first heard that God wanted to deliver the Jews from their affliction. Until that moment, they had lived in Egypt two hundred and ten years, while the decree called for four hundred years in a foreign land. There was a discrepancy of one hundred and ninety years. It was not the right time! However, by appearing to Moses on a lowly bush, God hinted that the *Shechinah*'s exile and distress made up for the remaining years of affliction.

Thus we praise God during the Haggadah reading: "Blessed is He Who keeps His pledge to Israel; for He calculated the *ketz*, the end of the bondage, in order to do as He said to our father Abraham at the Covenant between the Parts." As the numerical value of *ketz* (קץ) adds to 190, the exile concluded by as many years earlier on account of the suffering of the *Shechinah* which descended to Egypt with Jacob and his children.[13] Accordingly, the next paragraph begins with *vehi she'amdah* – the Divine Presence is what stood by our fathers and us during all the exiles.

Thus we lift the wine cup to recall our individual obligation to elevate the *Shechinah* through our *mitzvot*. No one should feel unworthy of such a grand mission, saying to himself who am I that I should deserve to participate in uplifting the holy *Shechinah*?[14] *Le'akama Shechintah Me'afrah* – to elevate the *Shechinah* from the dust, can be accomplished by each one of us when we perform God's commandments for no ulterior motives except

12 Rashi, Exodus 3:2

13 Zohar, Terumah 134a

14 R. Elimelech Mi'Gradzisk, Terumah 93

le'shem shamayim, for the sake of heaven, where the word *le'shem* (לשם) stands for *Le'akama Shechintah Me'afrah*, to elevate the *Shechinah* from the dust.[15] ■

The Splitting of the Red Sea and Creation

The Midrash suggests that God made a conditional clause with Creation that later in history the Red Sea should reverse its natural course and split to accommodate the miraculous passage of the Jewish People.[16] This break with the laws of nature stands in contradiction to King Solomon's teachings: "Whatever has been is what will be... There is nothing new beneath the sun!"[17] In other words, whatever we observe around us has been set in place during the six days of Creation. Nothing is new. In which case, the Splitting of the Red Sea contradicts this age-old dictum.[18]

At the same time, the Sages teach that at twilight on the first Shabbat eve, God created ten entities which, in the right time, would intervene to defy the course of nature.[19] As they came into being during the final moments of Creation, they do not conflict with the above declaration by King Solomon.

These ten objects are:

- The mouth of the earth, which eventually swallowed Korah and his fellow conspirators. [20]
- The mouth of the well provided water for Israel in the Wilderness.[21]
- The mouth of the donkey rebuked Balaam.[22]
- The rainbow served as a sign of the covenant between God and mankind.[23]

---

15 R. Mi'Aftah, teacher of R. Elimelech Mi'Gradzisk

16 *Bereshit Rabbah* 5:4

17 Ecclesiastes 1:9

18 *Maor Vashemesh, Shevi'i Shel Pesach*

19 BT *Avot* 5:8

20 Numbers 16:32

21 BT *Taanit* 9a

22 Numbers 22:28

23 Genesis 9:13

- The manna fell from heaven to feed an entire nation for forty years.[24]
- The staff which Moses used to perform the miracles in Egypt.[25] According to Rabbinic tradition, it belonged to Adam and was transmitted through the generations to Moses. The Four Letter Divine Name was engraved on it.
- The *Shamir*, a small worm which, according to the Mishna, split large stones as it crawled on them.[26] Since no sword or iron – symbols of war – could be used to hew the stones for the construction of the Temple, the symbol of peace – the *Shamir* took the place of conventional tools.
- The script is the form of the Hebrew alphabet.
- The inscription is the instrument used by God to engrave the Tablets of the Ten Commandments, which were miraculously "written on both sides."[27]
- Finally, the first Tablets were created then, but the second ones were later carved by Moses. Some say destructive spirits,[28] Moses's grave,[29] and the ram of our forefather Abraham were also created at that memorable twilight. And some say also the tongs. According to this view, God provided man with the original pair of tongs with which to hold red hot metal and make others.

It is evident that these unnatural elements were appended to the created world at the last minute to deflect any argumentation at the time of their occurrence in the future. When the earth shall open its mouth to swallow Korah and his followers, it will be an unnatural event, but within the framework of Creation. Still, why does God intentionally step in to change the natural order?

God created numerous worlds with their individual angels and galaxies in order to be acknowledged and praised by these entities. Our material

24 Exodus 16:15

25 Ibid., 4:17

26 BT *Sotah* 48b

27 Exodus 32:15

28 For a mystical explanation on why these "*mazikin*" (demons) were created without a physical body, see R. Yosef Gabay, *A Bridge to Heaven: A Collection of Classic Commentaries on the Torah*, New York: Targum Press, 2004, 315.

29 For an explanation on why Moses's tomb remains unknown to this day, see ibid., 410.

world is equally part of God's initial Creation. Here too, all created beings should recognize God in the material surroundings. However, on account of the physicality of our environment, the danger of forgetting the Creator over time is real. Man will err in thinking that nature sustains itself without any intervention. As the sun naturally rises and sets, man might mistakenly conclude that there is no Master. With the passage of time, the animal and inanimate worlds would too, reach the same erroneous conclusion, thinking that the world is ownerless. When the six days of Creation were followed by the holiness of the Shabbat, all created beings strongly sensed the presence of their Creator. The Divine Light which descended upon the world on that first Shabbat eve was a strong reminder to all of the Oneness of God. In time, the renewal of that light was essential in preventing man and all other beings from forgetting their Master.

During the twilight, on that first Shabbat eve, when the holiness of Shabbat began to descend upon the world, God created these additional material entities so that all physical elements in the created world would always regain the spirituality of the first Shabbat eve and never come to forget the Creator. Thus inanimate objects such as stone tablets would, at the right occasion, become the recipients for spiritual commandments. The donkey, who symbolizes physicality, would open its mouth to fulfill the wishes of its Creator. The ram of our forefather Abraham ran to be sacrificed when it reminisced on that Divine Light it experienced during its birth at twilight time. The Divine Light of that first Shabbat eve would make a lasting imprint on all beings so as to never forget their Creator.

However, with the passage of time, the Red Sea had forgotten the presence of the Creator and refused to split open for Israel. God reminded the sea of the conditional clause He had stipulated at Creation: "and toward morning the water went back to its power [*le'eitano*] as the Egyptians were fleeing toward it."[30] The Hebrew word *le'eitano* is interpreted as *le'tenao*, to its initial condition. That was sufficient for the Red Sea to experience again the Divine Light that pervaded the world on the first Shabbat eve and to fulfill the wishes of its Master.

30 Exodus 14:27

Moreover, when the sea split, the heavenly light of the first Shabbat descended upon the Red Sea. Thus the Torah describes the unusual reaction of the Egyptian army: "and the Egyptians were fleeing toward it [the Red Sea]."[31] They should have been running away from it not toward it! It is on account of the awesome beauty of the original Divine Light which descended upon the Red Sea. As they were attracted to its splendor, the Egyptians ran toward it, but the Divine Light would not tolerate them because of their abject immorality. ■

The Eternity of the Exodus

The Torah commands each one of us to relive the Exodus as if we personally left Egypt. How does the Torah raise such an expectation when none of us dwelt in Egypt?[32] Yet, the Torah's message is eternal and it applies to all future generations. Similarly, the first of the Ten Commandments states in the present form: "I am Hashem, your God, Who has taken you out of the land of Egypt, from the house of slavery."[33] This being a statement of eternal belief in One God, and the foundation of Jewish faith, it also invites us to feel as if we recently were saved from bondage.

The Midrash sheds some light on this extraordinary concept. The souls of Am Yisrael who walked out of Egypt to stand by Mount Sinai and receive the Torah were the root *neshamot* of all Jewish generations to come.[34] Moses, unequivocally informed Am Yisrael of this supernatural condition: "Not with you alone do I seal this covenant and this imprecation, but with whoever is here, standing with us today before Hashem, and with whoever is not here with us today."[35] As to re-emphasize this idea, Moses adds: "Only beware for yourself and greatly beware for your soul, lest you forget the things that your eyes have seen..."[36] Without hesitation, the Torah reminds every Jew of what he witnessed with his own eyes at Sinai.

---

31 Ibid.

32 R. Shalom Noach Berzovsky, *Netivot Shalom*, Pesach 14

33 Exodus 20:2

34 *Lekach Tov*, Deuteronomy 29:9

35 Deuteronomy, 29:13

36 Ibid., 4:9

Likewise, when Am Yisrael walked out of Egypt, it was an assembly of all Jewish souls that would ever exist. Thus any written story or injunction present in the Torah is directed not only to past generations but also to ours. This explains why these commandments are expressed in the present tense: "so that you remember the day of your departure from the land of Egypt all the days of your life."[37] It is therefore, our duty to awaken the spiritual experience of the Exodus and of the Sinai Revelation, as if we were physically present at these historical events.

This idea is emphasized in the wording of the Hagaddah: "Hashem brought us out of Egypt not through an angel, not through a seraph, not through a messenger, but the Holy One, Blessed is He, in His glory, Himself." In reality, what difference would it make whether we were delivered by an angel or by God? It is because the messenger's action is limited and can benefit only the individuals of that particular generation. On the other hand, God's intervention will endure to benefit future generations. On account of God's eternity, the deliverance will equally be eternal, making Egypt's Exodus an everlasting experience.

Likewise, the Ten Commandments which were uttered at Sinai, along with the thunder and the flames, the sound of the *shofar* and the smoking mountain, remain eternal as we testify during the services of Yom Kippur: "Forever, Hashem, is Your Word established in the heavens."[38] Accordingly, Moses urges Am Yisrael to always remember: "the day that you stood before Hashem, your God, at Horeb, when Hashem said to me, 'Gather the people to Me and I shall let them hear My words...'"[39] As this revelation is eternal, it renews itself daily in the same manner that Creation does. It is said that whenever the Holy Baal Shem Tov revealed hidden mystical Torah secrets to his disciples, they had the merit to hear the same thunder that accompanied the Giving of the Torah at Sinai.

Furthermore, just as we elaborated on this concept where the deliverance affects every future generation and must be eternally relived, so does the divine decree imposing the exile apply to every generation. The

37 Ibid., 16:3

38 Psalms 19:15

39 Deuteronomy 4:10

message conveyed by: "Know with certainty that your *zaracha* [offspring] shall be aliens in a land not their own – and they will serve them and they will oppress them,"[40] equally applies to every Jew. This is hinted at by the singular form of the word *zaracha*. Just as a seed must first rot under the dirt prior to sprouting into a strong fruit tree, so must a Jew experience the exile in order to relive the joy of redemption. The benefits of achievements may not be savored unless they were preceded by substantial depravations. Exile represents the *raison d'être* of redemption. The psalmist's words strongly convey this idea: "When God will return the captivity of Zion, we will be like dreamers."[41] It is a reference to Joseph who suffered many years in Pharaoh's dungeons before becoming king of Egypt. Likewise, when God will end the captivity of Am Yisrael, they will realize that all the retributions were for a salutary purpose.

Moreover, during the morning services, we praise God for renewing Creation: "In His goodness renews every day, constantly, the work of Creation." [42] What is gained by this approach? It seems that it would be logical to let Creation pursue its course and naturally continue its existence as set in the first six days. Why is it necessary for God to intercede every day to renew Creation? Such is God's design so that the forces of renewal which He releases will equally affect the Jew to renew his commitment to God.

In Egypt, the Jews' moral decline matched the corruption of their host culture. Leaving Egypt meant spiritual revival. The celebration of the Exodus implies abandoning the immoralities of alien cultures. It is an eternal struggle which the Jewish individual can win by rejecting evil ways and promoting good. These two distinct ways of worship, *sur merah* and *asei tov*, must be part of a Jew's life each day. Thanks to this approach, Israel's final redemption will be assured. ■

The Light of Redemption Shines from the Exile

Judaism's fundamental tenet is enclosed in the words of the Mishna: "This world is like a lobby before the World to Come; prepare yourself

40 Genesis 15:13

41 Psalms 126

42 *Birkat Yotzer Ohr*

in the lobby so you may enter the banquet hall."[43] From the Torah point of view, any worldly activity which does not lend itself to this objective is to no avail. A Jew's material and spiritual pursuits must, at the end of the day, lead to the successful fruition of this tenet. Judaism's *hashkafa* stands in stark opposition to the commonly expressed idea that "we only live once, let's have fun."

The good, the retributions and struggles along with the exiles and their persecutions, are all part of the hallway that leads to the fulfillment of God's Plan for the Jewish individual and people. It is a world so sublime that even the ministering angels, the Seraphim and Ofanim, cannot inherit.

Although this world may look disappointing, in reality there is no evil that comes from God. Yet, there is a disturbing paradox which many struggle to comprehend. As the Sages tell us that God's intent in creating the world consists in bestowing His goodness upon all creatures, where do we find the realization of this goal?[44] On the contrary, we seem to be constantly surrounded by evil. The wars, the diseases, malnutrition and torture are rampant. So are social injustice, poverty and a persistent glorification of falsehood. Where then is the unhindered flow of divine kindness upon the world? We must conclude that God's infinite bounty cannot be dispensed in our finite and material world. We live in the lobby, the hallway that leads to the World to Come, where material restraints are absent. On the tortuous journey of this world, we ready ourselves to partake of God's endless bounty.

Still, we cannot silently sweep under the rug a burning question. Why is it necessary to suffer in order to achieve some form of *tikkun*? How does suffering atone for one's spiritual failures to somehow close the gap between these failures and our obligations to God? The Arizal explains that it is easier to rectify a sin linked to a single body part than one that is performed by the whole body. For instance, if one ignores the dietary laws or the mitzvah of *tefillin*, he could easily repair that failure as only one body limb was involved. But when a person sins with his

43 *Avot* 4:21

44 R. Luzzato, *Mesilat Yesharim*, Introduction

mind, eyes, heart and entire body as is the case with illicit relations and/ or unwarranted seminal discharge,[45] then the *tikkun* requires a full bodily and mental subjugation, uniquely experienced through physical suffering. The divine response is based on the idea of measure for measure, where heavenly justice is dispensed to reflect man's flawed conduct. Then, a sort of *mesirut nefesh*, self-sacrifice, accompanied with an abnegation of the self, takes place under the burden of pain. When a person is healthy and prosperous, he rarely contemplates his shortcomings, much less the path to amend them. The exile, where an individual is subjugated to the unscrupulous will of tyrants, is a *tikkun* for this specific type of spiritual blemish.

When God informed Abraham that: "Know with certainty that your *zaracha* [offspring] shall be aliens in a land not their own – and they will serve them and they will oppress them,"[46] He was hinting at the tight correspondence that will always exist between exile and the severe sin caused by *zaracha*, uncalled-for seminal discharge. Thus on the eve of Yom Kippur, we begin the prayer services with a *piyyut*, a poem dedicating our inner selves to God as a *tikkun* for this very sin: "*Lecha Eli teshukati*" – "towards You my God, is my fervent yearning, to You are consecrated my mind and my emotions, my spirit and my soul… to You are dedicated my flesh and my blood, my eyes and my thoughts…"

The anticipation of redemption and the enduring tragedies of the exile are intertwined with the existence of the Jewish People.[47] Since the dawn of Creation, it seems that the Jewish People had been chosen for a life of suffering and maltreatment. Moreover, this fatalistic concept finds support within the very first words of the book of Genesis. Says the Midrash: "when the earth was astonishingly empty," alludes to the first two exiles under Babylon and Persia.[48] The third and fourth exiles under Greece and Rome are also hinted at in the continuation of the same verse: "with darkness upon the surface of the deep." It is evident that long before the history of man had begun, the fate of the Jewish

45 The Zohar (Genesis 38:9) describes this sin as one of the worst in the Torah, for which there is almost no possibility of repentance, unless one does so forcefully.

46 Genesis 15:13

47 R. Berzovsky *Netivot Shalom*, Pesach, Exile and Redemption

48 *Midrash Rabbah* 2:4 on Genesis 1:1

People had been sealed. Likewise, adds the same Midrash, the concept of redemption existed since the early moments of Creation: "and the spirit of Elokim hovered upon the surface of the waters." This is the Mashiach about whom it is written: "The spirit of Hashem will rest upon him – a spirit of wisdom and understanding."[49]

Similarly, during the famous Covenant between the Parts in which God promised the Land of Canaan to Abraham's descendants, the Midrash suggests that "and behold – a dread! Great darkness fell upon him"[50] equally alludes to each one of the agonizing exiles in addition to the enslavement by ancient Egypt.[51] In conclusion, the Jews' existence is mostly identified with pain and suffering. We cannot help but wonder what is the purpose of this unsettling destiny?

Unlike the last three exiles, marked first by the Prophets' rebukes and warnings to the Israelites, the exile in Egypt could not have been a divine retribution over Israel's sinful conduct. When they arrived in Egypt, Jacob and his offspring, who numbered seventy, were all righteous. Yet, by the time they left Egypt, the Jews had sunk to the mystical forty-ninth level of impurity due to their long exposure in an immoral culture. So, what was gained from that exile?

The objective of the Jews' enslavement in Egypt was to redeem a myriad of holy souls who ended up in that land following the sins of Adam and the generations of the flood and the dispersion (the Tower of Babel). These souls were entrapped within the confines of the *sitra achra*[52] in Egypt and could only be freed through the presence and suffering of the Jewish People. Similarly, the Zohar reveals that during the Covenant between the Parts, God stipulated that Bnei Yisrael would have to go through a purifying process by suffering in a foreign land in order to become the Chosen People. Abraham accepted that condition, since it guarantees his progeny to live closer to God and to inherit a life of eternal bliss in the World to Come.[53]

---

49 Isaiah 11:2

50 Genesis 15:12

51 *Bereshit Rabbah* 44:20

52 Literally, "the other side," it is a kabbalistic appellation of the forces of evil.

53 Zohar I, 83a

This being the case, how then do we justify the subsequent exiles under the oppressive rules of other tyrants? When we consider the Prophets' gloomy warnings to Israel, it is clear that the latter's sins were the cause to their exiles. However, based on the Midrash, Israel's fate was sealed even before their sin.

With regard to the Jewish nation, God had set at the time of Creation two separate calendars with their specific historical events.[54] In His infinite wisdom, God had anticipated Am Yisrael's disobedience to the Torah and plotted a tumultuous and painful path through which they can still achieve the *tikkun olam*, perfection of the world. A much smoother and different historical path was equally drafted should Bnei Yisrael choose to live in accordance with God's Will. So, according to the first plan, God had decreed when the Beit Hamikdash would be built, when it would be destroyed, when the Jews would be exiled and when they would be redeemed. According to the second plan, if Israel would not sin, the Temple would not be destroyed and they would not go into exile. Yet, it is hard to come to terms with this justification. Why is it necessary for Israel to be displaced through force and suffering from its land for so long?

The pain endured in exile is likened to the lobby where one readies himself before entering the banquet hall. Just as the Egyptian bondage acted as a spiritual purification process prior to receiving the Torah, so too, the other exiles act as a preparatory step toward the ultimate benefit of man, namely, the Messianic Times and the World to Come. So, when one considers this life an end in itself, he is rightly shocked at the apparent degradation of the Jewish People. But when we look at this world as a jump start toward the eternal life of true bliss, then there is no longer any room for astonishment.

For the shortsighted, it is indeed a horrific destiny that has befallen the Jewish People. As to the distinguished thinker who strives to acquire the wisdom of the Torah, this world is viewed as a passageway, a preparatory stage to a life of eternity. To the seasoned eye, all suffering, while difficult, has a purpose. Just as light cannot exist without darkness, and

54 HaMagid Mi'Koznitz on *Be'er Hagolah* by the Maharal

good cannot be appreciated without evil, so too absolute salvation will have no meaning without exile and its consequences. The greater the suffering, the greater will be the ultimate revelation. Exile is essential to reaching the ultimate goal.

When Moses pleaded with Pharaoh to let the Jewish People go, the Egyptian ruler instead increased the yoke of slavery on the enslaved Israelites. Now, not only did the people have to build continuously, but they had to collect straw to make their own bricks, and still fill the same quotas as before. Shocked by this cruel reaction; Moses asked God: "My Lord, why have You done evil to this people?"[55] God replied: "Now you will see what I shall do to Pharaoh." The denouement of this dramatic event between man and God strengthens the liaison that will always exist between suffering and redemption. God's answer to Moses is that light will shine forth only from the depths of darkness. As we all know, it is only after the darkest part of night that dawn comes. When He told Moses, "Now you will see," God was informing him that the miraculous destruction of Pharaoh's army at the Red Sea, along with the forthcoming historical Sinai Revelation, were commensurate with the Jews' suffering. One could not happen without the other.

Likewise, the painful assaults of the past century will be proportionate in their suffering to the grandiosity of the Messianic Revelation which the world shall soon witness. This, by analogy, is the story of Joseph the dreamer. After spending many years as a forgotten slave in the dungeon, he becomes king of Egypt and saves the world.[56] So it is alluded to in Psalm 126: "When God will return the captivity of Zion, we will be like dreamers." When the long-awaited return to Zion finally comes to pass, the recollection of the past oppressions of the exile will swiftly fade away and seem like a bad dream.

God, in His infinite wisdom, which transcends time and space as well as man's most refined intellectual prowess and emotions, has allocated to the souls of those whom He cherishes the highest spiritual realms in the World to Come. This is the ultimate redemption, which cannot be

55 Exodus 5:22
56 Genesis 47:25

attained without the burdensome price of affliction. In his famous and often misinterpreted prophecy, Isaiah foretold that the nations and their kings would contrast their former scornful attitude toward the Jews with new realization of Israel's grandeur:[57]

"Behold, My servant [God's servant, the people of Israel] will succeed; he will be exalted and become high and exceedingly lofty... He was despised, and we [the nations of the world] had no regard for him [the people of Israel]. But in truth, it was our ills that he [the people of Israel] bore, our pains that he carried – but we [the nations of the world] had regarded him diseased, stricken by God, and afflicted... His chastisement was for our benefit and through his wounds, we were healed."[58]

When Israel's exile is finally ended, the nations will marvel that such people could have survived so much persecution. When the time of redemption arrives, Israel will astonish the nations by its exaltedness, just as it had once been shockingly degraded. A healthy man will never appreciate the benefits of his health unless he was once terribly sick, just as one who had known hunger will always appreciate a good meal.

In Jewish tradition, the day begins at sunset and not at sunrise. Thus the Shabbat always starts on Friday evening instead of Saturday morning. This is significant as it highlights a perspective of life that reflects the experience of the Jewish People. With patience and confidence, we walk through the night before we celebrate the day. The seed that the farmer sows must first rot in the dirt before sprouting forth into a healthy fruit tree. Although everyone treads upon it, growth continues. Such is the nature that God imprinted in His Creation. True light cannot be experienced without darkness. Just as darkness precedes the day, so must anguish come before solace. First, Israel must journey through the night. Then it will faithfully await the promise of a brighter day.

Consequently, the conclusion of the Midrash above points to the spirit of the Mashiach surging at the end of the lengthy and almost hopeless exile under Edom (Christianity). Since the dawn of history, no

57 Christian doctrine is substantially based on this misinterpretation.

58 Isaiah 52:13, 53:3–5

nation has ever so unjustly suffered as the Jewish People has under Edom. As we are fast approaching the Messianic Era where all nations will acknowledge God's Oneness and abolish idol worship, this grandiose revelation rightly trails the seemingly endless exile under Edom's yoke. ■

SEARCHING INSIDE THE HOLES AND CRACKS

One of the most basic Pesach regulations consists in searching for and eliminating the *chametz* on the eve of the fourteenth of Nisan, one day before the Passover celebration. Armed with a lit candle, we check for bread crumbs through the holes and cracks of the house walls. The underlying lesson behind this exercise is to focus our attention on burning a most pressing form of *chametz*, namely, our *yetzer harah*, the evil inclination.[59] Just as we are urged to remove all traces of *chametz*, we are required to eliminate all nuances of evil from our heart. In the same manner that *chametz* can be visible, hidden or absorbed within the walls of a utensil, evil can be found within us at different levels. Although one may religiously guard himself from sin, it is possible that he will unknowingly harbor a specific type of evil. One's *tikkun* will not be achieved as long as the veiled evil remains deeply entrenched within him.

As every *neshama* descends to this world for a particular *tikkun*, it could well be that one's *tikkun* is to free his heart of a deeply rooted and dormant evil. Although an individual might attain high spiritual rungs, his success in God's worship will not be complete until he burns this other type of *chametz*.

Additionally, this ritual calls on the young Bar Mitzvah adult, who stands on the eve of his fourteenth year, to examine his commitment to Judaism. In the same way that the Jewish People became a Torah nation on the eve of Pesach, this young man stands to proclaim his pledge of allegiance and to define his identity. But first, on the eve of the fourteenth, he too must burn the silent *chametz* that hides within his heart.

Is it possible to target the evil that is brewing inside the heart? How can one ascertain its nature? It is with the aid of our individual *neshama*

---

59 R. Berzovsky, *Netivot Shalom*, Pesach 2

which King Solomon likens to the candle's flame. "A man's soul is the lamp of Hashem, which searches the chambers of one's innards."[60] A person's *neshama* will guide him to recognize his weaknesses and determine the evil which drives them. Likewise, the Torah that one studies constitutes life's best beam of light: "For a commandment is a lamp and the Torah is light; and reproving discipline is the way of life."[61] Thus with the aid of a lit candle, we are urged to search for the *chametz* and examine our heart.

A story is told of a wood chopper who realized that he could spend a lifetime cutting the forest's trees without even making a dent in its vast horizons. So he set the forest on fire to clear the needed area. Similarly, it is not enough to remove the *chametz*; it must be burned along with one's *yetzer* in order to walk with sanctity into the joyful celebration of Pesach.

No one is privy to the evil thoughts entertained by another person. Like the deep holes and cracks, they are hidden from the eye. Yet, they can be a formidable adversary in the service of God. The thoughts define man's essence and determine his character and conduct. If they are polluted, they will certainly affect their carrier. Cain murdered Abel, his brother, because he let jealousy settle in his heart – a seemingly harmless feeling.[62] So, the preparatory steps for Pesach require that we burn this lingering type of *chametz*, the malevolent thoughts.

The duties of the heart are the foundations of Judaism. They include our faith in God, loving and revering Him, as well as clinging to God's teachings. The rejection of anger and the negation of haughtiness equally belong to the duties of the heart. About these hidden sentiments the Sages warn: "Jealousy, envy and the pursuit of prestige will destroy man's potential to happiness."[63] On Pesach eve, with the help of a lit candle, one must walk through the dark chambers of his heart to burn away the veils which hinder his closeness to God. Indeed, one can savor the perfect taste of freedom when he is no longer bound to his evil.

---

60 Proverbs 20:27

61 Ibid., 6:23

62 Genesis 4

63 *Avot* 4:28

As the Children of Israel dwelt in Egypt for over two hundred years, their spirit and heart became polluted by the abject immorality of the local culture. Witchcraft, idol worship, illicit conjugal relations, widespread social injustice and tyranny were the traits of ancient Egypt. The Jews were not spared and sank into the mystical forty-nine levels of impurity.[64] The fiftieth level is described as a point of no return. The state of moral corruption becomes irreversible. There is a five-day lapse between Shabbat Hagadol (before Pesach) and Pesach during which God – in His infinite kindness – released ten levels of holiness each day upon Am Yisrael to cleanse them from the defilements of Egypt and to prepare them for their redemption. The days preceding Pesach are opportune for repentance leading to a higher state of holiness.

Halachically, the physical burning of *chametz* implies a total abandonment of leavened bread for a few days. It is null, void and treated like dust. Similarly, as Pesach approaches, one must demonstrate his love for God by shunning physical desires which impair God's worship. The sentiment of love, when correctly applied, will elevate an individual to sublime spiritual spheres, but when used to advance selfish pursuits, love can bring him down. Just as the line between leavened and unleavened bread is fine – after all it is the same recipe of water and flour – so the way this character trait is utilized can build or destroy a person. Unbridled thirst for women, money, and expensive food and wines is a recipe for failure, while the love for God, the Torah and one's family will bring spiritual serenity.

The Sages of the Mishna teach that objectionable character traits force an individual out of this world.[65] What do they mean? How can a person find himself brushed to the outer rims of the planet? God put man in this world with an implied expectation of proper conduct. Being created in God's image, it is only natural that he adopts an inherent code of decency. But when he succumbs to his physical desires, then he breaches the framework of moral behavior, he is said to have removed himself from the world. The search for *chametz* is a time for introspection to revisit and refine our character traits. ■

64 *Maor Vashemesh* – Shabbat HaGadol.

65 *Avot* 2:16

THE EMUNAH OF SHEVI'I SHEL PESACH

The splitting of the Red Sea took place on Shevi'i shel Pesach, the seventh day following the Exodus from Egypt. On that day, Pharaoh's armies pursued and reached the Israelites, wanting to force them back into slavery. The Israelites feared for their lives when they saw their tormentors approach. It was only then that they cried out to God. Following the unprecedented and historical miracle where Pharaoh's entire army drowned, the text describes the people's immediate reaction: "Israel saw the great hand that Hashem inflicted upon Egypt; and the people revered Hashem, and they had faith in Hashem and in Moses, His servant."[66]

It seems that the Torah is praising Israel's expression of faith after they witnessed God's extraordinary intervention on their behalf. What is so commendable about this reaction? Wouldn't everyone feel a strong surge of faith after observing this incredible divine act?[67] In general, faith is an abstract feeling which implies the absence of a concrete setting or eye-witness testimony. So, why does the Torah positively qualify Israel's expression of faith? Having witnessed such a grand miracle, it would only be expected for Israel to strengthen its faith in God. Besides, in an earlier encounter between Moses and the Children of Israel, the latter did express their belief in God: "And the people believed, and they heard that Hashem had remembered the children of Israel and that He saw their affliction…"[68] What can a renewal of faith at the Red Sea add at this time?

Faith can be broken down into three separate levels. A faith based on rational observance is of a lowest form. One would strongly rely on his intellect to decide what to believe. A higher level is a faith felt in man's heart. The characteristic of this kind of belief makes it far superior to the first type as one does not uniquely rely on his reasoning. However, the greatest degree is found when faith pervades one's bodily limbs as in: "All my bones shall say, Hashem, who is like You."[69] It is common to see people run away with fear from an animal such as a dog, notwithstanding the strong faith

66 Exodus 14:31

67 R. Berzovsky, *Netivot Shalom*, Shevi'i shel Pesach 1

68 Exodus 4:31

69 *Nishmat Kol Chai*

in God which they feel in their heart. This is due to an inadequate faith which does not pervade all their body. Joseph was thrown by his brothers into a pit filled with snakes and scorpions. He was saved thanks to his righteousness and faith in God. It is not the snake which causes harm; rather, it is man's sin.

When Moses was given the task to deliver Am Yisrael from Egypt, He argued that the Jews would not believe in his mission. God reassured him that it would not be so, because they were the descendants of Abraham, Isaac and Jacob who showed great faith in God. On this account alone, every Jew believes in God. If sometimes it is not the case, it is because his faith is dormant due to the many materialistic layers which accumulated over long years of exile and exposure to foreign cultures. This individual is compared to an overcast day when although the sun cannot be seen, it is certainly there. Throughout our turbulent history, there were Jews who acted against Torah regulations to their hearts' desire. Yet, when they were forced to choose between death and the enemy's religion, they sacrificed their life without hesitation. This unnatural conduct is due to a faith that is deeply rooted within their soul. This is described as the first or the second level of faith which depends on one's intellectual observations or emotional experiences. It explains why the Jews worried when they saw the Egyptians at their pursuit. They had not as yet embraced the highest level of faith which permeates all their body.

However, as the miracle of the splitting of the Red Sea unfolded, Bnei Yisrael's faith surged to the highest point, pervading all their bodily limbs, truly living these words: "All my bones shall say, Hashem, who is like You." Consequently, every year, on Shevi'i shel Pesach, the *ohr*, light, of ultimate faith in God descends upon Am Yisrael. It is the opportune moment to relive the level of *emunah*, faith, that Bnei Yisrael experienced on that momentous occasion. Shevi'i shel Pesach is the Rosh Hashana *la'emunah*.

Thanks to *emunat ha'evarim*, a faith that pervades the bodily limbs, Am Yisrael can oppose the evil forces which promote atheism and immorality. This was the motto of ancient Egypt. Pharaoh arrogantly declared: "Who is Hashem that I should heed His voice to send out Israel? I do not know Hashem."[70] In parallel with this slogan of atheism, Egypt was also

70 Exodus 5:2

known as "*ervat ha'aretz*," a land of abject immorality. These two distinct aspects of evil can only be brought down by their counterparts, namely, unrestrained faith in God and *kedusha* – holiness. These traits were both acquired by Israel at the splitting of the Red Sea and, soon after, at the Sinai Revelation. The true appreciation of Godliness is achieved only through unrestrained faith. ■

WHY DO YOU CRY OUT TO ME?

Soon after the Israelites left Egypt, Pharaoh and his fearsome army pursued and reached them. The Israelites literally found themselves sandwiched between the enemy and a raging sea. As they were very frightened, they cried out to God. Attempting to comfort them, Moses explained that God would surely save them. At that moment God addressed Moses asking: "Why do you cry out to Me? Speak to the Children of Israel and let them journey forth!"[71]

Many Torah Sages struggled with this question. What is Moses supposed to do at a time of imminent danger if not to pray?[72] Besides, do we not find that the Jews were rescued from Egypt thanks to their prayer? "Then we cried out to Hashem, the God of our forefathers, and Hashem heard our voice and saw our affliction… Hashem took us out of Egypt with a strong hand…"[73]

There are times when prayer is to no avail as the prosecuting forces in heaven are just too overwhelming.

When the Israelites stood by the Red Sea, they were not deserving of any miracles. In heaven, the prosecuting angels argued before God against Israel: "The Egyptians worshipped idols and the Israelites worshipped the same idols!" they rightly claimed. "So why should You, Hashem, save these and drown the others?"

---

71 Exodus 14:15

72 R. Berzovsky, *Netivot Shalom*, Pesach 5

73 Deuteronomy 26:7

On account of this irrefutable argument, we often find passages in the Talmud describing the splitting of the Red Sea as a "difficult decision." Indeed, it was a hard choice for God. His propensity to give and act with kindness is restrained by our shameless deeds. The prosecuting voices are sound and it is difficult to weaken their case. Hence, God tells Moses: "Why do you cry out to Me?" This is not the right time for prayer as it will not help. Rather, the only act that will justify your salvation is: "Speak to the Children of Israel and let them journey forth!" Tell them to show their full *bitachon*, reliance on Me, by stepping into the raging waves. In fact, the merit of reliance on God overrules any heavenly prosecution, regardless of the latter's strength of arguments. Notwithstanding man's sins, the trait of *bitachon* in God triggers heavenly compassion to flow upon the world.

Although the redemption from Egypt was initiated by Bnei Yisrael's prayer, it was equally mitigated by God's promise to Abraham: "and afterwards they will leave with great wealth."[74] As it were, God had to redeem Israel regardless of their spiritual decline. But at the crossing of the Red Sea, no promise was made that Israel would be miraculously saved. Israel had to earn the merit. God urged Moses: "Let them prove their trust in Me by journeying into the waters, effectively drawing upon them an extraordinary miracle."

This situation is illustrated by an analogous story. Once, a traveler camped at night around the king's palace. To the guards who found him in the middle of the night he begged: "Please do not beat me as I belong to the king's immediate entourage."

The guards held him till the morning, and then they brought him to the palace. "You claim you know me?" asked the king.

"I do not, your majesty." He replied. "However, I relied on your compassion to save myself." Realizing that the traveler relied on him, the king ordered the guards to free him without harm.

Considering the eternity of the Torah, the message equally applies to us today on an individual basis as well as on a national scale. Even under

74 Genesis 15:14

the direst conditions, one's prayers will not be turned down if he displays full *bitachon* in God. In Persia, under the threat of annihilation poised by Haman, Esther turned to God: "My God! I call to You daily, and You do not answer, and I call also at night, and there is no silence with me [as I continue to cry out]."[75] The heavenly prosecution blocked her prayers until she invoked the reliance of our ancestors: "Our forefathers placed their trust in You and You saved them."[76] Through trust in God, a person uproots himself away from the daily natural boundaries. In turn, God responds with unnatural outcomes.

Since God had promised Abraham that He will redeem the People of Israel from Egypt, the Exodus had to take place at all costs, notwithstanding Israel's spiritual failure. Unlike most situations involving God's relationship with man, breaking Egypt's bondage was an initiative taken by God. In kabbalistic terms, this is described as *it'aruta dil'eilah*, an initiative taken from high above. But at the Red Sea, the initiative justifying God's salutary intervention had to originate from Am Yisrael. This is described as *it'aruta dil'teitah*. It is up to man to justify a beneficial divine response. In this case, a verbal commitment is not sufficient. To be effective, one must show his reliance on God with deeds such as self-sacrifice. Hence, God interrupts Moses's prayers: "Why do you cry out to Me? Let the Children of Israel demonstrate their *mesirut nefesh*! Let them step into the waters!"

So, even today, when a Jew is deeply entrenched in the mystical forty-nine levels of impurity, he can still draw upon him the light which descended upon the world during the miracle of the Red Sea. At any moment, he can show his readiness to fulfill God's recommendation: "Speak to the Children of Israel and let them journey forth!" *Bitachon* in Hashem is a key to overruling prosecuting angels and to awakening God's compassion. ■

THE POWER OF THE HOLY TONGUE

We are taught that the Children of Israel were saved from Egypt in the merit of three conducts which they scrupulously upheld during their

75 Psalms 22:3
76 Ibid., 22:5

long exile: they did not change their names, their language and their dress code.[77] How is it possible to live in a foreign land for two hundred and ten years without adopting the local culture and language?[78] What is so great about maintaining their mother tongue and names? We shall equally endeavor to clarify the Sages' claim that after the sinners are entombed, they forget their name.[79] What is the relevance of this detail?

Since the Torah was given in Hebrew, we define this language and its twenty-two characters as holy. This is quite unusual because the holiness of a language is generally identified by its substance rather than by its alphabet. When a person guards his speech from slander, from lies and deceptions, from mockery and from vile expressions, then he is said to speak a holy language. Until the epoch of the Tower of Babel and the dispersion, Hebrew was the only spoken language. When God scattered that generation across the entire earth, He built new languages upon the combination of the twenty-two Hebrew characters. As a result, any language can be holy based on its contents.

In fact, the criteria for a holy tongue rest with what goes in as well as what comes out of the mouth. The Sages caution to first make sure that prohibited foods do not go through our mouth.[80] Kosher speech and food are the main ingredients of *brit halashon*, the covenant of the language. When *brit halashon* is carefully observed, then the destructive forces are kept at bay. Otherwise, the *yetzer* is unleashed upon the individual who defiles this covenant. In fact, even the nature of one's prayers and Torah study are open to question as they are at the mercy of the *yetzer*.

Likewise, the name given at birth to a Jewish child represents a formulation of these Hebrew characters and is linked to the celestial origin of that child's *neshama*. A sinner who defiles his speech and disregards the dietary laws draws upon him the moribund influence of the destructive forces. Eventually, these forces manipulate the letter combinations which originally composed his name to the point where it is no longer identified with his *neshama*. When the sinner leaves this world, he cannot recall his

77 *Vayikrah Rabbah* 34:5

78 *Maor Vashemesh, Ramzei Pesachim*

79 *Eliah Rabbah, Shelah Hakadosh, Siddur Nahar Shalom*

80 *Tanah Debei Eliahu Rabbah* 26

name at the onset of his judgment – a self-incriminating evidence to a sinful life.

Despite the hard life the Jews led in Egypt, they maintained the holiness of their language. In their daily interactions, they used Hebrew, their mother tongue, and upheld the dignity of the speech as they categorically avoided lies and hypocrisies. Since the holiness of their names was maintained, they kept the destructive forces at bay. So the combination of the Torah letters which formed their individual names remained unchanged. Throughout the exile, their names continued to reflect the purity of their *neshama*. Although the Israelites had adopted many immoral mores of the host culture which led them to low levels of impurity, the merit for preserving their speech, name and modest dress code justified their redemption.

The Zohar adds that in Egypt, the language was also in exile.[81] Elaborating on this idea, the Arizal explains that the forces of evil gain their sustenance from the holiness of Israel when it becomes flawed. Pharaoh, whose Hebrew name reads into *ha-oref*, the neck, held a strong spell over the five sounds which emanate from the throat. Pharaoh attempted to defile the holiness of Israel's speech by disseminating lies and evil discourse. In doing so, he would enslave the Israelites physically as well as spiritually, since a disreputable language would bring them under the influence of evil. Thus when asked to save the Jews from their bondage, Moses argued: "Behold! I have sealed lips, so how shall Pharaoh heed me?"[82] Moses argued that since the language is also in exile how can he make any impression on Pharaoh?

During those long years of harsh bondage, Am Yisrael fought against the immoral influences of Pharaoh and upheld the holiness of their language and names. It is in this merit that they were redeemed. The holiness of the speech was equally redeemed from the Egyptian exile. This is the reason we are commanded to recount the story of the Exodus. By reciting the Haggadah on the eve of Pesach, and through this verbal ritual, we purify and extract our speech from the grip of the *yetzer*. The observance

81 Zohar II 25b
82 Exodus 6:30

of this Torah commandment stands to protect our speech against base and heretical discourse.

During the Hagaddah reading, we tell the story of the Sages who were reclining at the Seder in Bnei Brak and discussed the Exodus all that night until their students said to them: "Our masters, it is daybreak and time for the reading of the morning *Shema*." The essence of acknowledging God's Kingship rests with the reading of the *Shema*. It can best be fulfilled with a holy speech which renews itself every year on Pesach eve. On that night, the students experienced that holiness which yearly descends from heaven and urged their teachers to recite the *Shema*. It was the best moment to accept anew the yoke of heaven.

In our narrative of the Exodus, we further state: "Had not the Holy One, Blessed is He, taken our fathers from Egypt, then, we, our children, and our children's children would have remained enslaved to Pharaoh in Egypt." It was thanks to God's help that we maintained the holiness of the language and shook away Pharaoh's destructive hold on the power of speech. Consequently, on this night, it is our duty to highlight the value of dignified speech to the four sons: the wise, the wicked one, the simple and the one who is unable to ask. Pesach eve is the propitious moment to refine our speech, as the language's holiness reaches its pinnacle. Thus we begin by reciting the Haggadah, the story of the redemption, merited by Israel for preserving the *brit halashon*. ■

Shavuot

SHAVUOT

The intrinsic nature of the Land of Israel is to instill meekness into its inhabitants. It is known as Eretz Canaan, the land of the subdued, for Canaan translates into hachna'a, *submission. That is the reason God gave this land to the Jewish People, so they can readily develop the attribute of humility, a prerequisite to living according to the Torah. This sheds some clarity on the Midrash's assertion that the Torah was given on Mount Sinai as well as on Mount Moriah.*[1] *Located in Israel, it is the area in Jerusalem where the Beit Hamikdash was built and where the Sanhedrin would meet. According to this Midrash, God miraculously displaced Mount Moriah to join Mount Sinai. Now, the criteria for receiving the Torah – humility and the ability to maintain this attribute, respectively represented by Mount Sinai and Mount Moriah – is put together for the benefit of Israel.*

---

1 *Yalkut Reuveni*, Yitro 50

A GIFT OF POTENTIAL FROM SMOL AND RAHAV

The Midrash reveals that, prior to giving the Torah to the Jewish People, God first offered it to the children of Seir (Esau), then to the children of Ishmael, and that both nations declined the offer.[2] This idea is derived from the following verse: "Hashem came from Sinai – having shone forth to them (Israel) from Seir, having appeared from Mount Paran, and then approached with some of the holy myriads – from His right hand He presented the fiery Torah to them [Israel]."[3] Seir and Paran are the lands of Esau and Ishmael. On the other hand, the Talmud relates that God offered the Torah to all the nations of the world and they rejected the offer.[4] In fact, the nations of Seir and Ishmael encompass, on account of their importance, all the seventy nations of the world.[5] As these two nations rejected God's offer, then the remaining nations followed suit.

Exactly whom did God address in His attempt to offer the Torah?[6] We do not know of any prophet who represented Esau or Ishmael. The Zohar answers that God offered the Torah to Smol, Esau's angel.[7] The logical assumption is that the people of Edom will follow their leader and agree to live by the Torah.

> As Smol wanted to know what is written in the Torah, God replied: "You shall not kill."[8]

"The nature of my rule depends on killing," replied Smol. "The wars which I am to wage and the conquests I live for heavily rely on the sword; I cannot agree to the Torah," he added.

Then, Smol begged God to turn His attention away from him and to approach Jacob's children. Smol went a step further; as an incentive to Am Yisrael, he willingly donated his only attribute of holiness. It is thus

2 *Eicha Rabbati* 3:1
3 Deuteronomy 33:2
4 BT *Avodah Zarah* 2b
5 *Torat Chaim, Avodah Zarah* 2b
6 R. Friedman *Shvilei Pinchas*, Shavuot 5768
7 Zohar, Balak 192a
8 Exodus 20:13

written: "having shone forth to them from Seir." God took the holiness which shone over Seir and gave it to Israel.

Next, God approached Rahav, Ishmael's angel, with the same request. Again, the logical assumption is that if Rahav accepts the Torah, then the children of Ishmael will too abide by it.

A similar dialogue took place in heaven.

"What does the Torah require?" asked Rahav.

"You shall not commit adultery," was the answer.

"Woe to my lot if I should submit to this rule!" exclaimed Rahav. "How could I become fruitful and spread across the globe if I accept the Torah? Please, Hashem, give the Torah to my second brother Isaac. As an incentive, take back the special attribute of holiness which I inherited, and give it to Isaac's children."

It is thus written: "having appeared from Mount Paran." God took the holiness which shone over Ishmael and gave it to Israel.

According to this exchange, it is obvious that God skipped over the content of the Torah when introducing it to Esau's angel and to Ishmael's angel. He only mentioned two restrictive commandments, albeit cardinal in their nature. What about the remaining six hundred and eleven commandments? What is the reason behind this approach? Likewise, we shall endeavor to elaborate on the two attributes of holiness of which both angels willingly divested themselves for the benefit of Israel.

The Mishna in Avot asks:[9] "Who is strong? He who subdues his personal inclination, as it is said: 'He who is slow to anger is better than the strong man, and a master of his passions is better than a conqueror of a city.'"[10] Elaborating on this teaching, the Maggid Mikoznitz[11]

9 *Avot* 4:1

10 Proverbs 16:32

11 *Avodat Yisrael, Avot* 4:1

suggests that every person comes to this world with his particular *yetzer*, evil inclination. Through some sincere introspection, it is easy to figure out the nature of one's *yetzer*. Then, a person should establish guidelines as a protection against it. Thus we find that different Talmud teachers were most careful with a specific commandment because it identified their weakness.[12]

In line with this clarification, Rabbi Tzaddok HaKohen of Lublin adds that the specific spiritual weakness of an individual is a pointer to his potential for overcoming that failure.[13] As an example, if one's tendency is to act with dishonesty in business dealings, then he undoubtedly garners within him the forces to rectify this inclination. Someone else might be prone to speaking evil about his friends and acquaintances. The strength to reverse this negative trend is part of his nature and waiting to be exploited. Since he was born with that *yetzer*, God granted him the necessary moral strength to reverse it. One's ability to excel in a behavior which opposes his weakness is guaranteed.

King Solomon wrote: "God has made the one as well as the other…"[14] Wherever holiness is manifest, impurity, its counterpart, is present in an equal intensity. Inversely, where immorality is rampant, it is a sign that the potential for ethical conduct is hidden right there. For God has created opposing forces for man's ultimate benefit. The continuous struggle can resolve either way, depending on man's exercise of his free will.

Consequently, Ahaz, King of Judah, who did so much evil in the eyes of God, was more prone to beget King Hizkiyahu who spread Torah across the Land of Israel. In his times, not one layman could be found from Dan, in the north, to Beersheba, in the south – all were Torah scholars. The concentration of evil is invariably paired with an equal intensity of goodness.

Likewise, Smol, Esau's angel, was predisposed to the evil of killing. That explains why, when asked what is written in the Torah, God replied:

12 BT *Shabbat* 118b
13 R. Tzaddok HaKohen of Lublin, *Tzidkat Hatzaddik* 49
14 Ecclesiastes 7:14

"You shall not kill." Nonetheless, an equal attribute of holiness was made available to Smol. So when God told Smol that the Torah reviles killing, He was informing him of his incredible potential for overcoming this evil tendency. It is through the balancing attribute of holiness within him, for "God has made the one as well as the other…" Not only did Esau's angel refuse to rectify his propensity toward killing, but he willingly gave away the attribute of goodness by which he could counterbalance his evil. That hidden potential for holiness was taken away from Esau's angel and passed on to Israel: "having shone forth to them [Israel] from Seir."

A similar scenario unraveled with Rahav, Ishmael's angel. When he asked God what is written in the Torah? He was told: "You shall not commit adultery." This was Rahav's inherent evil. God revealed to Ishmael's angel the ray of hope concealed within him, by which to counterbalance this evil. Rahav declined God's offer and eagerly transferred away his dormant light of holiness to Israel. Now, modesty in marital relations as well as family purity will strengthen the moral character of Israel. In offering his most valued asset to Israel, Rahav stayed away from the Torah.

The Zohar adds that, at Sinai, the Children of Israel acquiesced to the Torah by declaring "*na'aseh venishma*," – "we shall do and we shall hearken." Through this acceptance, they became immune to death and evil. The antidotes to the clutch of death and to the influence of evil are the very attributes of holiness Israel received from Esau and Ishmael. Esau's leaning to kill was countered by the unrestrained power of life, while Ishmael's inclination to debauchery was curbed by the absence of illicit relations – evil's main tool. Thus *na'aseh venishma,* respectively correspond to Esau and Ishmael whose names equally translate into doing and listening.

Israel lost that immunity to death and evil, immediately after the sin of the Golden Calf. The Talmud introduces this idea as follows: "Says Rabbi Simai; when Bnei Yisrael said '*na'aseh venishma*,' six hundred thousand ministering angels descended upon the six hundred thousand Israelites and crowned each one with two crowns, corresponding to *na'aseh venishma*. Following the Golden Calf sin, these crowns – Esau's spiritual radiance which neutralized death and Ishmael's attribute of goodness which reined in evil – were taken away from Israel. Rabbi Yochanan adds that they were instead given to Moses. Says Resh Lakish: 'In the Messianic Times, these crowns will be returned to Israel.'"[15]

What transpires from the above is that, first, God attempted to give the Torah to all the nations of the world before approaching Am Yisrael. Why then did our Sages establish a blessing over Torah reading which stands in contradiction to this fact? "Blessed are You Hashem, our God, King of the universe, Who chose us from all the nations, and gave us the Torah." It is clear that we were not the first choice!

In addition, this blessing follows a first blessing which reads: "Sweeten for us, Hashem, our God, the words of Your Torah in our mouth…" Uncharacteristically, Torah reading is the only mitzvah which requires the utterance of two blessings! Every other mitzvah is preceded with one blessing only! And why does the Talmud qualify this blessing as the finest of all blessings?[16]

The *Shelah Hakadosh* explains that at Sinai, Israel received the Torah in addition to the spiritual lights which represented the good sides of Esau and Ishmael.[17] These are Esau's attribute to neutralize his tendency to kill, and Ishmael's quality of goodness which reins in evil. This is the reason for saying both blessings. The first blessing corresponds to the Torah which God gave Am Yisrael. The second blessing corresponds to the spiritual lights taken from Esau and Ishmael. God foresaw that Esau and Ishmael, who represented all the other nations, would reject the Torah. When He offered it to Israel, He also gave them the spiritual portions of Smol and Rahav. We praise Him for choosing to give us the Torah portion from all the other nations. The Sages describe this blessing as the finest.

Although these spiritual attributes were taken away from Israel following their worship of the Golden Calf, Moses shares them back with Israel when Shabbat returns.[18] That is why Shabbat is described as one sixtieth part of *Olam Habbah* from where death and evil are absent.[19] It

15 BT *Shabbat* 88a
16 BT *Brachot* 11b
17 Yitro
18 The Arizal, *Mizmor Shir Leyom HaShabbat*
19 BT *Brachot* 57b

is not a coincidence that Shabbat is squeezed in between the days of rest of Ishmael and Esau (between Friday and Sunday). It weakens the *klipot*, damaging forces of Ishmael and Esau. Likewise, the additional minutes of holiness (*tosefet Shabbat*) that we add to the observance of Shabbat before it commences at sunset and following its conclusion at night time, contribute to the weakening of these *klipot* of Esau and Ishmael – the root *klipot* of all the seventy nations.

Furthermore, the Mishna teaches: "The world depends on three things – on Torah study, on the service of God, and on kind deeds."[20] In other words, if these three qualifications are not practiced, then the world will cease to exist. Ishmael inherited from his father Abraham the attribute of good deeds, for Abraham always upheld and preached the practice of *chessed*.[21] Esau inherited from his father Isaac the attribute of God's service, *avodah*. Although the Torah was given to Israel, the other two pillars of the world were missing to sustain it. Knowing that Smol and Rahav would not accept the Torah, God approached them first in order to transfer these spiritual foundations from Smol and Rahav to Israel so that the world's continuity may be assured. At Mount Sinai, Israel was chosen to uphold Torah study, the service of God, and to practice kindness. It was chosen to maintain the continuity of the cosmic system and to praise its Creator. ■

MOUNT SINAI'S LESSON IN HUMILITY

The most significant historical landmark in Creation is the Giving of the Torah to Israel. It is so because such was the divine design prior to creating the world. Still, if the Torah had to be given upon a mountain, there were certainly many mountains of reputable stature. Yet God chose to descend only on Mount Sinai. What is the relevance of this choice?[22]

As Mount Sinai was a small mountain, the Sages learn that God wanted to teach us the attribute of humbleness.[23] The Torah cannot settle in the haughty heart. The wise person who acts with arrogance loses his

20 *Avot* 1:2

21 Netziv, *Ha'Emek Davar*, VeZot HaBeracha

22 R. Friedman, *Shvilei Pinchas*, Erev Shavuot 5767

23 BT *Sotah* 5a

wisdom, says the Talmud.[24] The Torah is likened to water – in the same manner that water flows downward from a high point, so the Torah can only thrive with the humble.[25] In this regard, other high mountains are, by default, flawed on account of their prominence.

According to the Midrash, Mount Tabor and Mount Carmel vied for that glorious moment.[26] Interpreting King Solomon's words in "A man's pride will bring him low, but a lowly spirit will support his honor,"[27] the Midrash suggests that they allude to these two mountains' strong wish to partake in the Sinai Revelation. "A man's pride will bring him low" point to these two high mountains which were confident that God would descend on them, but were bypassed precisely because of their pride. "But a lowly spirit will support his honor" refers to Mount Sinai which remained humble.

Moreover, as to highlight His impatience with the conceited, God states that He cannot dwell in the same world as the haughty.[28] At the same time, the Sages explain that, were it not for God's help, no one can overcome his evil inclination.[29] Man is made of flesh and blood while evil is all fire, with lengthy years of pursuits to cause man's downfall. How can a human being who is left to his own devices win this battle? In sum, the arrogant person is abandoned at the mercy of his *yetzer*, with no divine help. So when God decided to give the Torah to Israel, He chose a low mountain to hint that meekness and the Torah are two inextricable entities.

Now, perhaps we can glimpse with better clarity at the Sages' teachings: "During the Sinai Revelation, God uprooted Mount Sinai and threatened to bury Israel under, if they would refuse to accept the Torah."[30] This dramatic event finds support in the words describing that awesome experience: "and they stood at the bottom of the mountain."[31]

24 BT *Pesachim* 66b
25 BT *Taanit* 7a
26 *Bereshit Rabbah*, 13:3
27 Proverbs 29:23
28 BT *Sotah* 5a
29 BT *Kiddushin* 30b
30 BT *Shabbat* 88a
31 Exodus 19:17

These seemingly superfluous words – for we already knew where they stood – hint at the above teaching. Still, was it necessary to present Israel with an ultimatum?[32] They had already accepted the Torah when they said: "*na'aseh venishma.*" The answer lies with the inherent humility represented by Mount Sinai. In reality, God knows that without humility, it is impossible to uphold the Torah. This message was convincingly conveyed, under the guise of a threat to Israel through the symbolisms of Mount Sinai. When humility is absent, so too is God's assistance. Consequently, the *yetzer*'s daily assaults remain unchecked.

The Rabbi of Ropshitz adds that the intrinsic nature of the Land of Israel is to instill meekness into its inhabitants.[33] It is known as "Eretz Canaan," the land of the subdued, for Canaan translates into *hachna'a*, submission. That is the reason God gave this land to the Jewish People, so they can readily develop the attribute of humility, a prerequisite to living according to the Torah. This sheds some clarity on the Midrash's assertion that the Torah was given on Mount Sinai as well as on Mount Moriah.[34] Located in Israel, Mount Moriah is the area in Jerusalem where the Beit Hamikdash was built and where the Sanhedrin would meet. According to this Midrash, God miraculously displaced Mount Moriah to join Mount Sinai. Now, the criteria for receiving the Torah – humility and the ability to maintain this attribute, respectively represented by Mount Sinai and Mount Moriah – is put together for the benefit of Israel.

Likewise, when Bnei Yisrael traveled to Jerusalem three times a year, they prostrated in front of Beit Hamikdash which was built upon Mount Moriah. It is the same spot where Abraham came close to sacrificing his son Isaac. This act of self-abnegation was passed throughout time and space to Abraham's children. They too will prostrate themselves, three times a year, in front of Mount Moriah, in an act of self-effacement.[35] The intrinsic nature of Mount Moriah enhances the attribute of humbleness in the character traits of Israel. That is the reason God moved this mountain to Mount Sinai at the Giving of the Torah.

---

32 *Tosefot, Shabbat* 88a

33 Shelach

34 *Yalkut Reuveni*, Yitro 50

35 *Baal Hatania*, Chanukah 276b

Furthermore, the Sages teach that God considers a good intention as if it were acted upon.[36] "That because you have done this thing [sacrificing Isaac], and have not withheld your son, your only one, that I shall surely bless you and greatly increase your offspring like the stars of the heavens."[37] From this declaration by the angel to Abraham when he nearly sacrificed his son, we learn that God treats a good intention as if it were fully realized. Since this conclusion was reached at Mount Moriah, God displaced this mountain during the Giving of the Torah to Mount Sinai, to emphasize that only with regard to Torah study and observance of its commandments does God treat a positive intent as a full act. This message is embodied by the adjoining of Mount Moriah to Mount Sinai where the Torah was delivered. The Rabbi of Ropshitz adds that the third Beit Hamikdash is being built daily in heavens by our prayers and *mitzvot*, as well as by our good intentions to do more.[38]

Humility testifies to one's constant awareness of Godliness in the world. It is a mean by which to maintain vigilant connection with God. Arrogance becomes simply irrational when one contemplates that the presence of the Creator of the universe pervades every space and molecule at all times. ■

GETTING READY FOR THE TORAH

On Shavuot, the Jewish People commemorate the Giving of the Torah which took place at Mount Sinai shortly after the Israelites left Egypt. Then, the Jews entered into a Covenant with God by accepting the Torah. Every year, the celebration of Shavuot implies a renewed commitment to the Torah's eternal principles.[39] In order to relive that historical experience, the Ohr HaChaim HaKadosh suggests three spiritual preparatory steps which he derives from the verse describing Israel's camping by Mount Sinai: "They journeyed from Rephidim and arrived at the Wilderness of Sinai and encamped in the Wilderness; and Israel encamped there, opposite the mountain."[40]

36 BT *Kiddushin* 40a

37 Genesis 22:16

38 *Zeraa Kodesh*, Ki Tetzei

39 Rav Chaim Shmuelevitz, *Sichot Mussar* 36

40 Exodus 19:2

Although Rephidim describes a location, it equally translates into a state of weakness, as the Israelites expressed doubts about God's presence in their ranks not long after the miraculous Exodus. In a stark reminder of their failure, God sent Amalek to attack them: "and because of their test of Hashem, saying, 'Is Hashem among us or not?' Amalek came and battled Israel in Rephidim."[41]

Likewise, our Torah acceptance must not be seeded with doubts; rather, it must be approached with steadfastness. The Torah requires vigorous devotion in order to comprehend its hidden secrets. From the point of view of the Torah, success in its study is not an option – it is a must. It can only be achieved through spirited determination, not laziness. For the Sages teach that the flame of the Torah finds its rightful place only by the individual who is ready to die for it:[42] "This is the Torah regarding a man who would die in the tent."[43] One must not regard this quality as desirable. Rather, it is a requirement which we learn from Yaakov Avinu who learned Torah for fourteen years at the yeshiva of Shem and Ever. Thanks to his boundless spiritual dedication, Yaakov Avinu never slept during these years.[44] Granted, as personal dispositions vary, not everyone is cut to becoming a Torah scholar. Still, *Rachmana liba bai* – God evaluates one's inner thoughts. He seems satisfied, as it were, with the sincerity of one's pursuits in this arena.

Similarly, the Talmud holds that to those who study Torah without ulterior motives, it is a prescription for life, while to those who study it for personal gains, it is as harmful as venom.[45] Here, the Talmud alludes to those who approach Torah study in a detached and nonchalant manner rather than with perseverance. It is more likely that they will harm themselves instead of benefiting from the Torah's endless blessings.

In the same vein, as a reward to those who learn Torah with devotion, God promises: "I will turn My attention to you, I will make you

41 Exodus 17:7-8
42 BT *Shabbat* 83b
43 Numbers 19:14
44 Rashi, Genesis 28:11
45 BT *Shabbat* 88b

fruitful and increase you."[46] As it were, God declares, He will walk away from all His occupations to reward you.[47] When we consider that on Rosh Hashana, God judges the entire world without stepping out of His usual routine, in this case however, He sets aside all other business to give full attention to the individual who learns Torah with resolve.

The second preparatory step for receiving the Torah is equally derived from the verse above. We know that the Children of Israel were in the Wilderness, why then, is it necessary to restate that they "encamped in the Wilderness?" Just as the Wilderness is a barren land, one who seeks the Torah should act with profound humility. The Torah will not settle with the haughty heart. As a case in point, the Sages suggest that, in the lengthy legal disputes between the academies of Hillel and Shamai, the *halacha*, legal ruling, was upheld like Hillel's disciples because they carried themselves with patience and reverence toward their opponents.[48] The Sages equally call on the person to be accommodating and flexible as a reed, rather than rigid as a cedar tree.[49] It is so valued an attribute that the Torah scroll is written with a pencil made of reed. As it were, the Torah letters agree to be written by the reed which is supple.

In line with this idea, we find that the Torah's wisdom refuses to coexist with the angry.[50] When Moses expressed his anger at the army officers who returned from the Midianites' battlefield, he momentarily lost his prophecy, to the point that the laws of koshering utensils, administered immediately following that event, were taught instead by Elazar the High Priest.[51] On account of his anger, Moses forgot these laws. The connection to Moses specifically forgetting these laws is that in the same manner that the nature of fire is to burn, and that of a knife is to cut, the Torah's nature is to depart from the angry individual. If one stretches his hand into a fire, he will burn, regardless of his intention. Likewise, one who gives in to anger, will invariably lose his Torah knowledge.

46 Leviticus 26:9
47 Rashi, ibid.
48 BT *Eruvin* 13b
49 BT *Ta'anit* 20b
50 BT *Shabbat* 30b
51 Numbers 31:21

One should not lightly treat the forgetfulness of the Torah. The resulting gap is immediately taken over by the forces of impurity. This is the reason a Jew can become *tamei*, impure, but not a gentile.[52] This also explains why only a Jew's corpse will bring impurity upon the house it lies in. The body is immediately assailed by the forces of impurity following the departure of the soul. The *kedusha* is replaced with *tumah.* The forces of impurity feed off the holiness of the Jew. Consequently, one who learns Torah and walks away from it later in life, or just forgets what he had learned, is substituting *kedusha* with *tumah.*

Finally, the third approach to ready oneself for the Torah is a program of study with a colleague. This, says the Ohr HaChaim HaKadosh, is implied in the last part of the above verse: "and Israel encamped there, opposite the mountain." At Sinai, the People of Israel were so united that God deemed them fit to receive His precious treasure, the Torah. It must be studied with a *chavruta*, a friend, rather than as a loner. The Torah was not given to individuals but to the whole people. The environment within the walls of the yeshiva must reflect this unity.

Elaborating on the exceptional merit of unity, the Talmud relates the greatness of the generation in which Rabbi Yehudah Bar El'ai lived.[53] The consideration they showed for each other was such that at any time six yeshiva students learned under the cover of one robe. They were extremely poor, but managed to protect themselves with one piece of clothing because they cared for each other. Praising the qualities of that generation, the Talmud states that it exceeded in spiritual greatness the generations of Moses and Joshua and of King Hizkiyahu, during which Torah study had spiked to unseen levels. As long as everyone worried about the well being of the other, then they all got by and achieved scholarly heights, but when everyone pulls the entire robe to himself, then no one benefits.

Moreover, the Maharsha sheds some light on the tragic plague that killed twenty-four thousand students of Rabbi Akiva.[54] It is because no one showed consideration for his fellow's Torah. The true honor one can

---

52 *Ohr HaChaim Hakadosh*, Chukkat 19:2 and Kedoshim 19:8

53 BT *Sanhedrin* 20a

54 BT *Yevamot* 62b

achieve is defined by his Torah knowledge. As Rabbi Akiva's students were mostly concerned with their personal spiritual success, respect and unity were missing. This unfortunate situation created a lack of harmony. Thus Rabbi Akiva warned the last five students he taught against such destructive behavior. Rabbi Meir Baal HaNess, Rabbi Yehudah, Rabbi Yossi, Rabbi Shimon bar Yochai and Rabbi Elazar ben Shamua spread the Torah across and beyond the Land of Israel. These five students brought the Torah back to Am Yisrael.

Just as sincere commitment and humility are key elements to our readiness for receiving God's Torah, we equally must strive toward an environment where unity and respect prevail, since the Torah was not given to individuals only. ■

TORAH STUDY RENEWS THE WORLD

The Midrash reveals that the Torah was created two thousand years earlier than our world.[55] It premises this statement on King Solomon's teachings: "I [the Torah] was then His [God's] nursling, I was then His delight day after day."[56] King David reveals that God's day equals one thousand years: "For even a thousand years in Your eyes are but a bygone yesterday."[57] We see that the Torah was within God's proximity, as it were, "day after day," for two thousand years. This being the case; how then do we reconcile all the major events known to us, such as the sin of Adam and Eve, and the advent of death?[58] These tragic human misfortunes resulted from Adam's disobedience which only occurred at a later time. Yet, it was already written in the Torah for two thousand years!

The Baal Shem Tov answers that the original Torah in heaven was written with a different and far superior combination of letters which are beyond man's perception.[59] The events which resulted from Adam's choice were not part of these permutations. It is only when God brought

55 *Bereshit Rabbah* 8:2
56 Proverbs 8:30
57 Psalms 90:4
58 R., *Shvilei Pinchas*, Yitro 5767
59 VeZot HaBrachah

the Torah to our world that a different letter formulation was grouped to describe newer events as they took place. So, when Adam sinned and death was decreed, the Torah introduced these occurrences through a worldly and more perceptible combination of letters which were not part of the original Torah.

However, in Messianic Times, Am Yisrael will merit to learn Torah in its purest form, as promised in Isaiah: "for Torah will come forth from Me."[60] Says the Midrash, a newer Torah shall come forth from God, the pure and sublime letter combinations which dwelt within God's vicinity two thousand years before Creation.[61] In those days of peace in the land, Israel shall delight in the study of God's Torah in its highest spiritual condition. In fact, it is this superior Torah that the souls of the righteous study with infinite delight in *Olam Habbah.*

Moreover, the Midrash suggests that every day, in the heavenly court, God issues a new halacha.[62] It is, says the Rav Mi'Afta thanks to this daily divine revitalization of halacha that, down here, the Talmud scholar finds the power to clarify and interpret Torah Laws which, in turn, re-energize the renewal of the world.[63] Thus the Talmud goes on to guarantee a portion in *Olam Habbah* to any student who learns halacha every day.[64] It is because this student regenerates the work of Creation through his dedication to Torah. During the Morning Prayer, we praise God with these words: "and in His goodness renews every day, constantly, the work of Creation."[65] For, if His Providence were removed from the world even for a moment, the world could no longer exist. Effectively, God constantly renews the world.

In line with this thought, we find that God concurred with a halachic ruling issued by Abraham, when three angels visited him on the third day of his circumcision. As the Divine Presence had first appeared to Abraham, the latter asked God to wait until he takes care of the three

60 Isaiah 51:4
61 *Vayikrah Rabbah* 13:3
62 *Bereshit Rabbah* 64:4
63 R. Mi'Aftah, *Ohev Yisrael* Toldot
64 BT *Niddah* 73a
65 Weekday Siddur, *Yotzer Ohr*

visitors, whom he thought were regular travelers. "And he [Abraham] said, My Lord, if I find favor in Your eyes, please pass not away from Your servant."[66] The Talmud deducts that *hachnassat orchim*, welcoming guests, is of greater importance than welcoming the Divine Presence.[67] Indeed, as God acquiesced to Abraham's request, it must be that on that very day this halacha – unknown so far – was issued in heaven for the first time. The same Midrash concludes that Abraham had access to the daily halacha which God renewed each day in heaven. "Because Abraham *heard* My voice, and observed My safeguards, My commandments, My decrees, and My Torahs."[68] Abraham was indeed privy to the divine voice.

When the three angels saw that God waited for Abraham to fulfill the mitzvah of *hachnassat orchim*, then they realized that their host, Abraham, was of greater spiritual stature than themselves.[69] While this halacha was clear to Abraham, it was unknown to them. In reality, how do we explain Abraham's unrestrained access to the inner corridors of heaven? From where does he get a ruling, to which even the angels are not privy?

The Arvei Nachal explains that Abraham was able to decipher the Torah letter combinations in their original form, thanks to his holiness and spiritual prowess.[70] This stands in line with the Talmud statement that Abraham fulfilled the entire Torah.[71] Abraham had access to the root status of the Torah in its purest character. That is how Abraham discovered the heavenly ruling whereby, *hachnassat orchim* is of greater value than welcoming the Divine Presence.

Furthermore, the Midrash relates that when Moses ascended to heaven to receive the Torah, the ministering angels attempted to harm him.[72] They were outraged by the presence of a human being in their heavenly spheres. At that moment, God caused Moses's face to resemble

---

66 Genesis 18:3
67 BT *Shabbat* 127a
68 Genesis 26:5
69 *Midrash Rabbah*, 48:14
70 Vayerah 1
71 BT *Yomah* 28b
72 *Shemot Rabbah* 28:1

Abraham. Then, God rebuked the angels: "Is this not the person who hosted you when you descended to earth and ate by his house?"

In fact, when the angels heard that Moses was ready to bring down the Torah, they wished to keep the Torah for themselves in its highest state where there is no exposure to the *yetzer* and material temptations.[73] Moses convinced them that the Torah he is taking is clothed into the letter combinations which befit the material world. It includes worldly commandments which give *nachat*, satisfaction, to God when Bnei Yisrael overcome their inclination and fulfill them. The angelic world had no business with the nature of these commandments. The injunction to respect the parents does not apply since angels have no parents. The warning against idol worship is also irrelevant in their environment. As God concurred with Moses, He changed his face to look like Abraham. God alluded to the halacha which Abraham discovered by reading the heavenly Torah in its purest format, something the angels were not able to achieve. Moses too had access to the original Torah and its lofty message. Just as the angels had experienced Abraham's prominence, now they should acknowledge Moses's greatness and relinquish their reservation. ■

A COMMITMENT TO ACCEPTING THE TORAH

When Bnei Yisrael stood at the foot of Mount Sinai, they made a most lasting impression when they declared: "Everything that Hashem has said, we will do and we will hearken!"[74] In general, people first listen, and if they agree to what is being proposed, then they proceed to live by it.[75] The People of Israel were ready to first live by God's word before analyzing the offer. In fact, says the Talmud,[76] a heavenly voice was heard wondering how the Children of Israel achieved such a spiritual perfection known only to the angelic world. Indeed, the angels are described as: "Bless Hashem, O His angels; the strong warriors who do His will, to hearken the voice of His word."[77] First, they perform God's command

73 Chatam Sofer *Torat Moshe*, Yitro 19:20

74 Exodus 24:7

75 R. Aaron Kotler, *Mishnat Rabbi Aaron* III, Shavuot

76 BT *Shabbat* 88a

77 Psalms 103:20

before they contemplate its content. At Sinai, Israel's spiritual stature rose to unparalleled heights present only in the angelic world.

Likewise, when the Jewish People were commanded to journey across the Red Sea, its waves were raging. Still, they obeyed God's instruction setting aside their rational objection. They did not know that the sea would split for their passage. This self-sacrifice will eternally stand before God, as a mark of honor for Israel.

So, when the People of Israel readied themselves to receive the Torah, they were on such a spiritual height that they deserved the title of "a most beloved treasure of all peoples and a kingdom of priests."[78] Had they maintained that spiritual greatness, they would busy themselves only with Torah study, and the word of the prophet Isaiah would have been fulfilled: "Foreigners will stand and tend your flocks and the sons of the stranger will be your plowmen and your vineyard workers."[79] Following the sin of the Golden Calf, only the Levites kept the title of priests. However, it remains God's ardent wish that every single Jew aspires to earn, through his efforts and ethics, the dignified title of "a most beloved treasure of all peoples and a kingdom of priests."

The Torah regulates our world as well as the heavenly worlds. The Talmud reveals that when the angels ask God on which day Rosh Hashana falls, He replies that "We have to wait until the Beit Din [court] in Jerusalem makes the announcement."[80] This is indicative of the power transferred from heaven to Israel thanks to the Torah. The latter covers all aspects of the Oral Law, to include all the debates that took place among the Sages. This is true even when the final halacha is not in accordance with that specific debate. King Solomon describes the Sages' debates in these words: "The words of the wise are like goads, and the nails well planted are the sayings of the masters of collections, coming from one Shepherd [God]."[81] Just as the nature of a plant is to multiply and to become fruitful, so do the Sages' discussions flow like an ever increasing water source.[82]

---

78 Exodus 19:5-6
79 Isaiah 51:5
80 Yerushalmi *Rosh Hashana* 1:3
81 Ecclesiastes 12:11
82 BT Chagiga 3b

The Tana Debei Eliyahu reveals that Moses asked God when the Sages would thoroughly clarify the halacha to the point where disagreements would cease.[83] God responded: "yield to the majority."[84] The well-established principles of deductions and the laws derived by means of Talmudic exegesis are an integral part of the Oral Torah which the Jewish People are urged to abide by: "According to the teaching that they [Sages] will teach you and according to the judgment that they will say to you, shall you do, you shall not deviate from the word that they will tell you, right of left."[85] Even if the Sages dictate that right is left and left is right we must not deviate, says Rashi. King Hizkiyahu refrained from begetting a son as he foresaw through *Ruach Hakodesh*, the Holy Spirit, that he would give birth to the wicked king Menashe. Notwithstanding the nobility of his motivation, he was rebuked by the prophet Isaiah for disobeying the Torah commandment to be fruitful. In accepting the Torah, there is no room for personal calculations, gains or pursuits.

When Moses went up to Mount Sinai, God urged him to return and warn the Children of Israel not to walk past a specific boundary of the mountain base:[86] "Descend, warn the people, lest they break through to Hashem to see, and a multitude of them will fall." Expounding on the word *rav*, multitude, the Mechilta[87] adds that even if a single Israelite falls, the Torah would not be given. God values the commitment of every person. Ever since, the acceptance of the Torah remains in the hands of each individual. All of God's Creation is justified by a single Jew who accepts the Torah. Consequently, the *Nefesh HaChaim*[88] suggests that the heavens and the earth will reverse to their original emptiness and darkness if the world stays without Torah: "Thus said Hashem, If My Covenant is not upheld day and night; I would not maintain the laws of heaven and earth."[89]

When the Children of Israel declared "Everything that Hashem has said, we will do and we will hearken," they essentially stated that it is

83 *Yalkut Tehillim* 12
84 Exodus 23:2
85 Deuteronomy 17:11
86 Exodus 19:21
87 Mechilta, Exodus 19:21
88 R. Chaim of Volozhin, *Nefesh HaChaim*, Shaar 4:11
89 Jeremiah 33:25

not the rationale of a religious precept that obligates a person to observe it, but rather the fact that it is a command from God. Even if a divine precept were a complete riddle to us, the obligatory character of the commandments would not be in the slightest degree impaired. In the final analysis, we follow the Torah's precepts or refrain from committing transgressions because it is the will of God. It is our mission in this world to be the servants of God with all our resources. In conclusion, the objective of Torah study is to live in accordance with its teachings notwithstanding our personal opinion. ■

MUSSAR IS A PREREQUISITE TO TORAH

When Moses addressed the Children of Israel during the course of the Ten Commandments, he urged them to develop their perception of shame:[90] "Do not fear, for in order to elevate you has God come; so that awe of Him shall be upon your faces, so that you shall not sin."[91] In the midst of thunder and lightning, Moses instilled in the hearts of Israel the feeling of shame of the Creator. It is through it that one will learn to fear God and to fulfill His wishes. This extraordinary thought can only be achieved through the study of *mussar* – Jewish ethical conduct. The Saba of Slabodka, an influential leader of the *mussar* movement, urged his disciples to employ every available ruse to study *mussar* as he believed that it is the foundation to accepting the Torah.

The trait of shame is the opposite of arrogance. The attribute of shame is tightly connected with intelligence – to such a degree that the two traits are interchangeable with each other. We see this regarding Adam and Eve, about whom it is written: "And they were both naked, the man and his wife, and they were not ashamed."[92] They were unaware of the idea of modesty until they ate from the Tree of Knowledge. The text then states: "And the eyes of both of them opened."[93] When they were able to distinguish between good and evil, their concept of shame,

90 Mechilta, Exodus 20:17

91 Exodus 20:17

92 Genesis 2:25.

93 Ibid., 3:7

until now absent, materialized. For this reason, all living creatures, with the exception of man, do not experience shame for they have no wisdom. They do not have the intellect to distinguish between right and wrong, good and bad.[94] It is only through the intellect and wisdom that one may acquire the truth and acknowledge the Oneness of his Creator and thus be ashamed of sin and exult in the good.

Since the quality of wisdom is so great, it must be paralleled in greatness by its related trait – shame. In general, the individual who has shame has knowledge, and the person who lacks knowledge will lack shame. Therefore, one should exert himself to act in accordance with the attribute of shame and employ wisdom until it is implanted in his soul to crown this trait above all his impulses. Through it, one attains many virtues and guards himself against all unbecoming qualities.

The trait of shame protects us from making transgressions. Often, man commits sins in private that he would be embarrassed to carry out in public. But the highest form of shame should be felt before the Holy One. You may ask: "How can I be ashamed before one whom I do not see?" In reality, God is present in the heart and mind of every person. One may attain various levels of shame by reflecting upon the greatness and omnipresence of God.

All people say and do many things in private, and think many thoughts. The main concern is that these do not become public knowledge. If all that they ever spoke and did and thought were known to others, they would be extremely embarrassed. How much more so must one feel ashamed before his Creator, who can see into the hearts and minds of man? If one is ashamed to transgress in public but does so in private, it is as if he "dupes" the Almighty, being ashamed before men and not before his Creator.

The trait of shame leads to humility and to modesty. It is a barrier against outrageous conduct which lowers traditional human values. It is,

---

94 *Orchot Tzaddikim*, a classical work on ethical behavior. This work appeared for the first time in Hebrew in 1581. The author is unknown, most likely on account of his humility.

indeed, the very opposite of arrogance. A society, in which the children are taught to appreciate the trait of shame, is a society that will surely flourish. So, during the awesome Sinai Revelation, Moses chose to highlight to the Children of Israel this lofty quality, because it leads to the fear of God, which is a prerequisite to accepting the Torah and to upholding its commandments. ■

RUTH – THE MOTHER OF ROYALTY

It is customary to read the Book of Ruth on Shavuot. It is the story of the Moabite who embraced the Jewish faith, and culminates with her giving birth to a son, Obed, who will father Jesse, the father of King David, the scion of Mashiach: "And so, Boaz took Ruth and she became his wife; and he came to her. Hashem let her conceive, and she bore a son… They named him Obed; he was the father of Jesse, the father of David."[95]

The link[96] between the story of the righteous convert and Shavuot, the celebration of the Torah, is hinted at in the Zohar on God's offer to the nations of the world.[97] "Hashem came from Sinai, having shone forth to them from Seir, having appeared from Mount Paran, and then approached with some of the holy myriads – from His right hand He presented the fiery Torah to them."[98] The Zohar explains that God first proposed the Torah to Esau's descendants. Not only did they reject the offer, but they pleaded that the Torah be given to Jacob's offspring. As an enticement, Esau offered Israel special gifts. When God turned to Ishmael, He heard the same refusal and was urged to give the Torah to Israel instead. Ishmael too offered gifts as goodwill to Israel.

What is the nature of the gifts donated by these nations to Israel? They are the holy *neshamot*, souls, who were entrapped within these nations since Adam's sin. These are the souls of the righteous converts, taken captive by the *sitra achra*, forces of evil as a result of Adam's failure. Over time, they will espouse Judaism and return under the wings of Torah.

95 Ruth 4:13-17
96 R. Levy Yitzhak of Berditchev, *Kedushat Levy*, Shavuot
97 Zohar, VeZot HaBeracha, *Eicha Rabbati* 3:1
98 Deuteronomy 33:2

Ruth, the holiest of these *neshamot*, will beget the Mashiach's soul. On Shavuot, we celebrate the Giving of the Torah and recall the mystical episode of freeing Ruth's *neshama* by reading the book of Ruth.

Moreover, the Talmud suggests that the Jewish generation who wandered the Wilderness under the leadership of Moses did not merit a place in the World to Come.[99] What exactly do the Sages mean by such a severe proclamation? After all, these people received the Torah at Mount Sinai! Undoubtedly, the highest spiritual aspiration of a Jew is to earn a place in *Olam Habbah*. The Jew's aspiration to inherit the World to Come rests with the *neshama*'s desire to dwell in God's proximity and benefit from the divine radiance. The *neshama*'s greatest bliss consists in discovering Godliness along with the fascinating destiny and origin of the *neshamot*. This is but a flavor of the unending spiritual delight to which the soul yearns. Although one might experience closeness to God in this life, thanks to Torah study and prayer, his achievement will pale when compared to the unrestrained spiritual happiness experienced in *Olam Habbah*. Man's ultimate greatness in life will be defined by the intensity of this pursuit.

The Wilderness generation experienced a divine closeness much similar to the bliss of the World to Come. They lived through the Splitting of the Red Sea and witnessed an incredible divine revelation. When they sang: "This is my God and I will build Him a Sanctuary,"[100] they actually pointed at a divine vision far greater than Ezekiel's vision of the celestial chariots.[101] Additionally, they received the Torah at Sinai and heard God's Voice. They were known as the generation of knowledge. Their concept of Godliness was infinite. In sum, they had experienced closeness to God similar to what they would come to discover in *Olam Habbah*. This is the underlying message the Sages conveyed when they declared that the generation of the Wilderness will not inherit the World to Come. They were merely describing the greatness achieved by the Jews of that generation. They had already experienced the infinite joys of *Olam Habbah*.

99 BT *Sanhedrin* 110b
100 Exodus 15:2
101 Rashi, Ibid.

On Shavuot, we read the book of Ruth which recounts the birth of Mashiach. It is to indicate that we are not yearning to the Messianic Era to bask in greatness and material wealth. Rather, our desire is to witness divine revelations and the fulfillment of Zechariah's prophecy: "God will be King over the entire world; on that day God will be One and His Name will be One."[102] ■

102 Zechariah 14:9

Rosh Hashana

ROSH HASHANA

Unlike man, where a thought is abstract and is likely to fade away, a divine contemplation is not lost and, eventually, translates into concrete result. Thus when the saintly Rabbi Akiva was tortured and killed by the Romans, and when the ministering angels wondered why would a holy man deserve such a tragic end, God silenced them: "kakh alta bemachshava" – "*such was My original thought. This is precisely the human being I considered creating [through the attribute of justice.]*"[1] *In the heights of* din, *austere justice, when the Romans tore the flesh of their virtuous victim with a comb of steel, Rabbi Akiva displayed unparalleled love of God uttering with his last breath* "Hashem Echad" – "*God is One.*" *Notwithstanding the terrible suffering – a manifestation of the divine harsh justice – Rabbi Akiva unwaveringly maintained his faith. Thus the original divine intention, when God sought to create the world through the attribute of justice, was not lost. It was later realized through Rabbi Akiva who served God as if man was ruled only with strict justice.*

1 BT *Menachot* 29b

GOD STILL ASKS MAN: "WHERE ARE YOU?"

As we celebrate Rosh Hashana, we also celebrate Adam's birthday. Since the world was created on the 25th of Elul, Adam was created on the sixth day which is the first of Tishrei or Rosh Hashana. Undoubtedly, this date shall always remain the greatest landmark in mankind's history.

However, this day is equally remembered for the dramatic spiritual fall of Adam who sinned through the Tree of Knowledge.[2] Adam disobeyed God's command and immediately lost his exalted spiritual status. Then God made an overture to Adam to repent by asking: "*Ayekah*" – "Where are you?" [3] To which Adam replied: "I heard the sound of You in the garden, and I was afraid because I am naked, so I hid." Adam wasted God's invitation to ponder on the enormity of his sin; instead, he played the blame game and proceeded to accuse Eve for misleading him.

Thousands of years later, it seems that this dramatic dialogue between man and God has yet to reach a fruitful conclusion. God is still asking man: "where are you?" Yet, man stubbornly continues to hide and to offer all kinds of excuses justifying his desires and pursuits. Unfortunately, it is only when tragedy strikes that man asks of God: "Where are You?" This question is often angrily directed at God when hard times strike. But when life is good, God's whereabouts are of no interest. And so, for years, man simply forgets God's existence to follow his heart's desires. When God intervenes to remind man of His presence, the latter is stunned and often outraged.

Let's attempt to understand the reason behind Adam's failure. How did he fall prey to an Evil Inclination that he did not know? The Primordial Serpent – a euphemism for Evil – was an outside force unknown to Adam and had no effect on his choice. It is only after Adam sinned that Evil became an integral part of man's essence, constantly impacting his judgment.

First, let us examine a couple of related statements our Sages taught as to the nature of Evil. "I, says Hashem to Israel, have created Evil, but

2 R. Friedman, *Shvilei Pinchas*, Ki Tetzei 5768
3 Genesis 3:9

I also have created its antidote – the Torah. If you apply yourselves with Torah study, you will not be misled by Evil."[4] The simple interpretation is that Evil represents an integral part of Creation and will constantly challenge man. However, thanks to Torah study, man will overcome his temptations. As the Torah is impregnated by a unique Divine Light, it will assist man in his struggle.[5]

The second Talmudic excerpt describes Evil as: "so a menacing force that seeks to destroy man, and, were it not for God's intervention, man would not withstand the challenge."[6] In other words, notwithstanding Torah study, Evil will still gain the upper hand and bring man down. However, it is only thanks to God's help that man is able to fight on. Obviously, there is a contradiction between these statements as to Evil's nature.

We will reconcile this discrepancy as follows: When Evil challenges man in a forward and revealed manner, it can be confronted and discarded through Torah study. But when Evil adopts a deceptive approach, such as when it suggests that a sinful act is truly a good deed that will please God, then, the protective benefits of the Torah will not help. In this dire situation, man definitely needs God's assistance.

Evil was never created to deceive man. Rather its mission was to openly challenge man. Had it remained faithful to this objective, man would have no trouble defeating it, thanks to Torah study. However, Evil rebelled against God, and proceeded to adopt treacherous ways to further its destructive agenda. It is this second face of Evil that trapped Adam and caused his downfall. The intended true nature of Evil could not have harmed Adam as it was not part of him yet.

Incidentally, this explains why the Primordial Serpent was cursed.[7] For we would argue: "Why should he be punished? Was he not created to challenge man? After all, he fulfilled his mission!" Evil was not true to

4 BT *Kiddushin* 30b

5 R. Luzzato, *Derech Hashem*, Chap II: "of all the myriad of created elements, only the Torah is imprinted with a Divine Light which can positively influence the *neshama* of the one who studies it."

6 BT *Kiddushin* 30b

7 Genesis 3:14

his ordained role. In his deceptive reasoning, he convinced Adam of the spiritual value in a sinful act followed by the act of repentance. "It is a sin for the sake of Heaven!" Adam was caught in a well-laid snare. When he realized that there is no sin for a good cause, it was already too late.

This unfolding drama is intertwined within God's address to the Serpent: "*ki assita zot*" – "because you have done this,"[8] where *zot* (this) also identifies the Torah as in: "*v'zot haTorah*" – "this is the teaching that Moses placed before the Children of Israel."[9] "Because you have distorted the Torah's message by contending that a rebellious act is a good deed, then accursed are you beyond all the cattle and beyond all beasts of the field."[10]

Hence, our Sages ask: "What is the slayer, a reference to Evil, guilty of? He is guilty of misleading man in believing that a sinful act is a noble deed."[11] Since he causes man to lose the World to Come, Evil is rightly labeled a killer.

Furthermore, commenting on the encounter between Yaakov Avinu and Esau, the Arizal explains that Yaakov was the reincarnation of Adam and that he, along with his descendants, were destined to accomplish the *tikkun* to Adam's failure.[12] At the same time, Esau was the physical embodiment of the Primordial Serpent. This explains Jacob's prayer: "Rescue me, please, from the hand of my brother, from the hand of Esau, for I fear him..."[13] He is not acting like a brother, but rather, like Esau, the Primordial Serpent who wants to convince me that a sinful act for the sake of Heaven is laudable.

So, what can we do to avoid falling into the treacherous snare of the rebellious Evil? King Solomon wrote: "One who has found a wife has

---

8 Ibid.

9 Deuteronomy 4:44

10 *Ohr HaChaim*, Lech Lecha, quoting the Baal Shem Tov's commentary on *Shabbat* 75a: "Of what is the *yetzer* guilty? He is guilty because he distorts the Torah's message (*mishum tzove'a*)."

11 BT *Shabbat* 75a

12 Vayigash

13 Genesis 32:12

found goodness, and has brought forth favor from Hashem."[14] The Bnei Issachar suggests that "a wife" alludes to the month of Elul.[15] The tropical duration of the astrological sign Virgo (virgin – [a wife]) is during the month of Elul. And "goodness" alludes to the days when God's goodwill abounds. Elul is the propitious time for *teshuvah*, repentance. This period is equally conducive to foiling Evil's deceitful approach and to carry that awareness with us throughout the whole year.

Many years have passed since the first Rosh Hashana when God created the world, and we stand on this awesome day ready to contemplate God's original call to mankind: "*Ayekah*, where are you?" We must unequivocally answer: "*Hineni*, I am here" rather than: "*Va'echaveh*, I hid." ■

God's Original Intent

Passover reminds us of the Exodus from Egypt. During Shavuot, we celebrate the historic Giving of the Torah. On Succot, we celebrate the miraculous shield God granted the nation of Israel as protective clouds hovered over them for forty years in the wilderness. Yom Kippur is the Day of Atonement when Moses descended from Mount Sinai with a second set of the Ten Commandment tablets.[16] So every Jewish holiday commemorates a unique and meaningful theme, except for Rosh Hashana which is known in the Torah as *Yom HaZikaron*, the Day of Remembrance. What is being remembered?[17]

As it were, on this day, God remembers His original intent of Creation. Then, He had considered creating man uniquely with the attribute of justice as indicated in the first words of Genesis 5:1: "on the day that *Elokim* created Man," where *Elokim* refers to the attribute of justice. This would mean that God would not tolerate any deviation from His

---

14 Proverbs 18:22

15 *Bnei Issachar*, Elul 1,3

16 Moses scattered the first set of the Ten Commandments when, after forty days in Mount Sinai, he returned to find the Jewish People worshipping the Golden Calf.

17 R. Shimshon Pincus, *Yom Bri'at Ha'adam*

law, or any rebellious act from man. He would respond instantly with punitive action. Instead, God created man with both the attributes of justice and compassion as reported: "And *Hashem Elokim* formed the man of dust from the ground."[18] Kabbalistic teachings hold that the divine name "Hashem" alludes to God's attribute of compassion while the name "Elokim" highlights strict judgment. In this case, both attributes are present, suggesting that God runs the world through a balanced approach of mercy and justice. God will await the sinner to change course and repent, rather than send immediate retribution.

However, unlike man, where a thought is abstract and is likely to fade away, a divine contemplation is not lost and, eventually, translates into concrete result. Thus when the saintly Rabbi Akiva was tortured and killed by the Romans, and when the ministering angels wondered why would a holy man deserve such a tragic end, God silenced them: "*kach alta bemachshava*," – "such was My original thought. This is precisely the human being I considered creating [through the attribute of justice.]"[19] In the heights of *din*, austere justice, when the Romans tore the flesh of their virtuous victim with a comb of steel, Rabbi Akiva displayed unparalleled love of God uttering with his last breath "*Hashem Echad*" – "God is One." Notwithstanding the terrible suffering – a manifestation of the divine harsh justice – Rabbi Akiva unwaveringly maintained his faith. Thus the original divine intention – when God sought to create the world through the attribute of justice – was not lost. It was later carried out through Rabbi Akiva who served God as if man was ruled only with strict justice.

This is the Adam that God wished to bring into the world, someone who would never compromise in his worship of God. It is the pristine definition of man as considered by God, then. Man would be constantly attached in thought and deeds to His Master. On this Day of Remembrance, God reminisces, as it were, on His original intent to create and rule man with the attribute of severe justice. Rosh Hashana is known as "*Yom HaZikaron*." It is also a day when we redefine ourselves to rise to the occasion and meet God's highest expectation of us.

18 Genesis 2:7

19 BT *Menachot* 29b

Our Sages tell of a fascinating episode involving the female deer and other animals in the forest. During times of drought, when the animals are thirsty they gather around the female deer to pray for rain. The deer puts her head inside a hole and roars violently. At that moment, God's compassions are aroused and rain comes pouring down. These dramatic events are alluded to in Psalms 42:1: "As the deer longs for brooks of water, so my soul longs for You, O God."[20] From this, we can conclude that the deer is a pious animal. Yet, it does retain its inborn characteristics and remains an animal. After it satisfied its thirst, the deer is content and shows no particular interest in greatness.

This story reflects man's attitude on Rosh Hashana. Knowing it is the Day of Judgment, he stands with awe before God. With tremor, his soul longs for God. Soon after, man reverts to his second nature, to his mundane pursuits. On *Yom HaZikaron*, as the Day of Remembrance, God searches how much of an Adam there is in each of us. How close we are to the original intent when God considered creating man. The challenge is to maintain one human face that clings to God throughout the year, not several that are shaped by the desires of each hour. ■

YOM HADIN: THE DAY OF CREATION

Rosh Hashana is also known as "*Yom HaDin*," the Day of Judgment. Yet, the Torah refers to it in different terms: "Speak to the Children of Israel, saying: In the seventh month, on the first of the month, there shall be a rest day for you, a remembrance with *shofar* blasts, a holy convocation."[21] This verse does not relate that man is judged on this day.[22] What led our Sages to conclude that on Rosh Hashana all creation stands before a heavenly court?[23] The answer lies with the awesome revelation whereby man was created on Rosh Hashana.[24] Although the world was created on the 25th of Elul, Adam, the ultimate object of Creation, was created six days later

20 See Rashi's commentary on this psalm.

21 Leviticus 23:24

22 R. Berzovsky, *Netivot Shalom*, Vol. II, "*Hayom Harat Olam*"

23 BT *Rosh Hashana* 16a

24 See the difference of opinion between Rabbi Eliezer and Rabbi Yehoshua in *Rosh Hashana* 10b

which is the first day of the month of Tishrei. On this historic anniversary, God revisits His work to reassert that the objective of Creation is fulfilled.

God re-examines the result of His efforts to determine whether it is right to maintain Creation. Are men's deeds too ugly to void the need for Creation or are they worthy to justify upholding it? Rosh Hashana is a day where all Creation – to include mankind, planets, animals and plants – is judged. It is not a day where punishment or reward is dispensed to those imbued with the freedom of choice. It is a day of re-evaluation. Should Creation continue or, God forbid, desist on account of man's conduct? This is likened to a king who invested billions of dollars to build a city with its complex infrastructure. A year later, he decides to pay a visit with his royal court to the inhabitants of the new city and evaluate their loyalty and gratitude. Do his subjects appreciate the king's goodwill and attention?

Likewise, the angels are judged on this remarkable day. Although they do not possess a free will to commit evil or perform good deeds, they stand with awe awaiting the outcome as all creation is re-evaluated. It is because the renewal of the Covenant between God and Am Yisrael is at stake on Rosh Hashana. Indeed, our Sages teach that the world was created for the sake of Israel and the Torah.[25] That the physical laws governing the heavens and earth will fall apart if the Jewish People abandon the Torah. On Rosh Hashana, this alliance awaits its renewal with trepidation.

Moreover, we find that Rosh Hashana is also qualified as *chag*, a joyous celebration: "Blow the *shofar* at the moon's renewal, at the time appointed for our festive day."[26] On one hand, everyone is anxiously aware of his pending judgment, yet he still celebrates with copious meals and elegant attire. This attitude stands in contrast to the awe-inspiring lyrics of the prayers recited on that day, and especially to the noticeable absence of the *Hallel*, excerpts of praise usually recited during other holidays.

This last point is underscored by the following dialogue that takes place on Rosh Hashana between God and the ministering angels:[27]

25 *Bereshit Rabbah* 1

26 Psalms 81:4

27 BT *Rosh Hashana* 32b

"What is the reason the Children of Israel do not sing to You on Rosh Hashana and Yom Kippur?" they ask.

God replies: "Is it acceptable that they sing at a time when I preside from My Throne of Justice and when the books of life and death are open?"

Undoubtedly, there is a stark incongruity between festive celebration and trepidation from a divine judgment. In reality, there is no inconsistency between both situations. Since Rosh Hashana represents a continuity of Creation and a renewal of the Covenant between God and the Jewish People, it is reason enough to rejoice. At the same time, we need to remain aware that the books of life and death are open. Those who wish to uphold God's order by abiding to the Torah laws have reason to celebrate as they partner with God to maintain Creation. It is this undertaking that defines the idea of "being written in the book of life." As to those who reject their responsibility in this Torah-World order, they essentially have forfeited their role within Creation. They are given free rein to live their life as they wish. The absence of divine participation in their life is synonymous to being inscribed in the book of death.

Furthermore, regarding Yom Kippur, how do we reconcile the fact that one can sin throughout the year only to be forgiven on this Day of Atonement? This unrestrained benevolence is in defiance to the concept of justice. However, when we realize that Rosh Hashana is less a day of dispensing justice to the individual and more a time for renewal, then the fear of favoritism is brushed aside. Is mankind's existence, and along with it, that of the universe justified? When, in His infinite way of dispensing justice, God concludes that Creation must continue, then it is reason enough to grant forgiveness and open a new chapter, so that man too can realize his mission within the cosmic system. ■

Beware of Blessings!

One of the most popular concepts of Rosh Hashana is the idea that people are judged on this day and inscribed in the book of life or the book of death. What does this mean? Are we not concerned with other issues or wishes such as good health, comfortable financial status, a harmonious marriage and children who make us proud through their behavior?[28]

In a discussion highlighting the heavenly approach to judging individuals on Rosh Hashana, the Talmud introduces two scenarios.[29] As a result of a community's evil conduct, the heavenly court determines that only a small amount of rain will fall on their farms. However, sometime later the community members repent. Then, as it cannot annul its original verdict, the heavenly court will make sure the small quantity of rain will fall exactly where and when it is most needed. Inversely, if a community changes its actions from good to bad, the abundant rain it was to receive will fall at a time and place where it is least needed. What we might conclude is that a sentence is not finalized on Rosh Hashana. The sentence could be reduced or worsened during the following days or weeks, depending on one's conduct. Apparently, the Day of Judgment does not seem to carry much weight as it is superseded by man's subsequent actions. In fact, this is precisely the case. Rosh Hashana is not the Day of Judgment in our usual understanding. This will only happen when man leaves this world; then, he will be judged for all his actions. Rosh Hashana does not deal with reward and punishment. Rather, it is concerned with life and death. Should one be given the tools by which to live or should he be offered other tools which will cause his demise? What are these tools? What is the definition of life and death?

The heavenly court may grant a person good health and livelihood so that he can find the time to perform acts of kindness and to study the Torah. This is life! Likewise, a person may be granted physical strength and wealth which he uses to satisfy his materialistic desires and pursuits. He expands his business to different cities, is caught in unending litigations, and is unable to make time for a spiritual retreat. He lives without Torah, *chessed*, and charitable acts. This is death!

Similarly, the righteous and wicked are no longer defined by their actions. Rather, they are defined by their respective aspirations, or lack of them, to best utilize the tools they are given in life. The righteous is

28 R. Shimshon Pincus, *Sifrei Chaim Vesifrei Metim*

29 *Rosh Hashana* 17b

alive because he maximizes his opportunities to find God. So, on Rosh Hashana, he is inscribed in the book of life. The wicked has no interest or ambition in searching for God. He is inscribed in the book of death, translating into a life devoid of any spiritual achievements or acts of kindness.

The Talmud teaches that there are no rewards in this world for performing the Torah commandments.[30] A gift from the infinite God will not find its rightful place in our finite world. The Giver is unlimited and the recipient is constrained by physical boundaries. The recipient is unable to receive and hold onto an immeasurable quantity of bounty. God's reward will only be dispensed to the living soul in the world of eternal bliss. Of course, the Torah is filled with mundane blessings and promises if we follow its instructions. These good things – such as rain, fertile land, peace and security – do not represent the final reward. They are vehicles to serve God through a life of ease and leisure. It is thanks to these blessings that we can delve into God's Torah and cling to His Presence in this world.

On Rosh Hashana, at the conclusion of the evening and morning services, we read Psalm 24 in which King David praises God's Creation: "The earth and all it contains are God's – the inhabited earth and all who dwell on it. For He founded it upon the seas and erected it upon the rivers." We learn that every object or idea at our disposition in this world should be used to find God. Wealth, when granted to an individual, represents a heavenly challenge. Will he enhance the cause of Good or strengthen the ranks of Evil? Will this person support the needy and Torah institutions and give *nachat* to God, or will he keep it all to himself? Our material possessions must be viewed as tools to satisfy a spiritual thirst that brings us closer to God. This represents the true definition of the meaning of life. This is the enduring message of Rosh Hashana.

Moreover, following the destruction of the Second Temple in Jerusalem, the Roman invaders handpicked ten Jewish righteous and put them to death in the most cruel manner.[31] To this day, they are known as the Ten Martyrs. As the governor's daughter admired the beauty of Rabbi Ishmael, the High Priest, she asked for his scalp. When the executioner's blade

30 BT *Kiddushin* 39b

31 *Otzar Hamidrashim* 439

reached the High Priest's forehead upon which his *tefillin* rested, Rabbi Ishmael screamed causing the heaven and earth to shake. He screamed a second time and the Divine Throne trembled. At that moment, the ministering angels pleaded before God: "Master of the Universe! You have revealed to Rabbi Ishmael all the hidden aspects of the Torah. Is this how You reward him? The cruelty of his death is unprecedented!" At that moment, a heavenly voice answered: "If I hear one more plea, I shall revert all of Creation to nothingness."

At first glance, it seemed that the ministering angels had a strong argument. How could the Heavens allow this brutal death for the High Priest who walked into the Holy of Holies on the most sacred day of the year, and who came out unscathed thanks to his piety? Besides, God's answer is hard to understand. Why would the world be destroyed?

The world's existence is premised upon mankind's prayers to God. It is man's thirst of connecting with God which assures the continuation of the world. The greatest danger to Creation in general, and to an individual in particular, comes when man feels fulfilled and convinces himself that he lacks nothing. At that moment, a schism occurs between mankind and God. Thus the objective of Creation becomes null and void. A continuous relationship between man and God is an absolute requisite. Man will not be allowed to sleep on his laurels and forget his Creator. Great achievements in education, science and wealth cannot supersede man's ultimate objective: to constantly seek God.

As long as the Jews brought their sacrifices to the Temple, the connection between man and God was satisfied. The animal being slaughtered, skinned and burned reminded man of his sins and he begged for forgiveness. But when the Temple was destroyed and the sacrificial offerings ceased, the Jews relied on the merits of their righteous and relaxed back. They did not feel the need to pray to God. Then, the world faced extinction once the aspiration to connect with God disappeared. In order to preserve the world, God instigated the horrid death of those ten righteous which awakened our pain and prayers for generations to come. Our cries guarantee the world's existence. Yes, sometimes the righteous too are written in the book of the dying, as a reminder that, in His worship, God will not tolerate our complacency. ■

The Shofar's Silence when Rosh Hashana Falls on Shabbat

Our Sages teach that when the People of Israel sound the *shofar* on Rosh Hashana, they invite God to walk away from His Throne of Justice and to settle instead upon the Throne of Compassion.[32] He will show mercy and issue favorable decrees rather than harsh indictments. This is alluded to in *Tehillim*: "Elokim [God] has ascended with the blast; Hashem, with the sound of the *shofar*." [33] God's Name, "Elokim" invokes the attribute of justice, while "Hashem" invokes the attribute of compassion.

Likewise, our Sages have prohibited blowing the *shofar* on Rosh Hashana when it falls on Shabbat. Their reasoning lies with the fear that one might come to carry a *shofar* on Shabbat from a private domain, such as a house, to a public domain, such as a street, and transgress the holiness of Shabbat, by performing one of the thirty-nine prohibited forms of work on Shabbat. It is evident from this ruling that they equate the holiness of Shabbat to the mystical effects of the *shofar* upon the higher spheres.[34] Just as the performance of the *shofar* commandment has the power to cause God to move from His Throne of Justice to the Throne of Compassion, so will the observance of Shabbat accomplish the same result. In heaven, the holiness of Shabbat is as efficient as the *tikkun*, the constructive effect of *shofar* blowing.

Furthermore, by refraining from blowing the *shofar* on Shabbat, we indicate our commitment to the dictate of our Sages who are empowered to uproot a Torah commandment when they see fit to do so: "According to the teaching that they will teach you and according to the judgment that they will say to you, shall you do; you shall not deviate from the word that they will tell you, right or left."[35] In this merit, God will recall the selfless dedication of Abraham and Isaac. Abraham represents the Written Torah since he had directly heard God's commandment to sacrifice his son. On the other hand, Isaac received his instructions only

---

32 *Vayikrah Rabbah* 29:3

33 Psalms 47:6

34 R. Friedman, *Shvilei Pinchas*, Rosh Hashana 5767

35 Deuteronomy 17:11

from his father. He could have argued that Jews do not sacrifice humans and that perhaps Abraham misunderstood. Instead, he went along and, without hesitation, acknowledged his father's prophecy. Therefore, Isaac, who followed his father's guidelines, is said to symbolize the Oral Law.

The Talmud states: "Says Hashem: 'On Rosh Hashana, blow the *shofar* so that I will recall to your favor the sacrifice of Isaac the son of Abraham.'"[36] As Isaac represents the Oral Law, we too acknowledge the greatness of our Sages' decision to refrain from blowing the *shofar* on Shabbat. This too is a major sacrifice on our parts on such an awesome day where life and death hang on the mystical power of the *shofar*. By following the footsteps of Yitzhak Avinu, we will merit that God will walk away from His Throne of Justice and dwell upon the Throne of Compassion. Indeed, as we pray on Rosh Hashana: "*Va'akedat Yitzhak le'zaro tizkor*" – it is our anticipation that God will remember Isaac's sacrifice, the personification of the Oral Law – for the benefit of his descendants.

Additionally, the Arizal explains that two types of judgments are issued on Rosh Hashana: the harsh (*kashia*) and the lenient (*rafia*).[37] It is the reason this holiday is celebrated over a two-day period. On the first day, our role consists in softening the strict heavenly verdicts through the *shofar* and the prayers. On the second day, we aim to sweeten the lenient judgments through a repeat of all rituals observed on the previous day, including the mitzvah of *shofar*. Praising the holiness of Shabbat, the Zohar adds:[38] "on this day [the Shabbat] all Divine judgments – the severe and the merciful – are subdued and will not affect the world."[39]

Although we refrain from sounding the *shofar*, both types of judgments are appeased through Shabbat's holiness. In essence, it seems that the compounding effects of Shabbat's sanctity and our prayers on this unique day generate a result similar to the *shofar* blowing. In reality, how do we explain the powerful effects of the *shofar*?

---

36 BT *Rosh Hashana* 16a

37 *Sha'ar Hakavanot*, Rosh Hashana III

38 Yitro 88b

39 As a symbolic supporting note, the numerical values of Shabbat and of *kashia* and *raffia* (in Hebrew) are equal.

Since Rosh Hashana is a day when everyone is being judged, we should be pleading for forgiveness by verbally confessing our long list of transgressions. Instead, God has commanded that we blow the *shofar* because of its higher mystical impact.[40] In heaven, prosecuting angels attempt to block our prayers on account of our lack of merits. Unlike the wording of prayer, the sound of the *shofar* is similar to a cry from the heart which is unknown to the angels and which they cannot stop. Only God recognizes that cry which rises undisturbed through the sound of the *shofar*.

Consequently, the Rambam adds the following to the laws of *shofar*: "One does not perform this mitzvah by blowing the *shofar*. Rather, it is through hearing the *shofar*. It is because God wanted to deprive the prosecuting angels from negatively affecting its performance, for they have an impact on anything that is worldly. It is not so with the *shofar*'s sound. It is likened to the sigh and feeling of repentance experienced by each person and which God accepts through the rising resonance of the shofar."[41] This is the silent cry that saved the Children of Israel from Egypt: "and the Children of Israel groaned because of the work and they cried out. Their outcry because of their work went up to God… and God knew."[42] Only God heard the sound of their affliction. The angels did not understand their plea. That is the reason they could not stop the Jews' prayer.

The anxiety that one experiences days and moments before a court appearance on a grave judicial case is quite understandable. The suspenseful ending could be devastating or beneficial. Similarly, as we walk into Rosh Hashana, we are in the dark as to the outcome of our judgment. The recipe for unequivocally spelling out this cloud of darkness is *teshuvah* and *achdut*, unity. In heaven, our personal readiness for *teshuvah* has more weight than the sum total of our deeds.[43] Such is the kindness of God. The book of life is readily open for the people who entertain a life of repentance and good deeds. God wants to know what a person intends

---

40 *Igrah DePirkah* 273

41 *Laws of Shofar* 1:1

42 Exodus 2:23

43 R. Nosson Wachtfogel in the name of the Saba Mi'Kelm, *Kovetz Sichot* on BT *Yevamot* 20a

to accomplish with his life. The answer to this question will determine in which of the two books one is inscribed.

Similarly, *achdut* is so dear in the Eyes of God that it possesses the power of reversing harsh decrees into blessings. Naturally, one must define *achdut* and act upon this definition, rather than simply wish for it. A few of its ingredients include showing respect for each other's *minhagim*, tolerating with grace the unfortunates, the uneducated and unlearned, and refraining from denigrating speech. Most importantly, it calls for erasing from one's heart feelings of superiority against any *Yehudi*.

Notwithstanding its mystical impacts, the *shofar* is equally a call to *teshuvah*, a return to Torah and a reassessment of our *middot*, our ethical conduct. ■

THE RECEIVING END OF GOD'S GOODNESS

On Rosh Hashana we pray to God to grant us life. As if a verbal promise is insufficient, we insist that He inscribes us in the book of life.[44] When one party wishes to donate a gift to a friend, no strings attached, the unwritten intent is usually adequate. Since the promise is not dependent upon any condition, it is not necessary to put it in writing. On the other hand, when the offer can be voided due to external pressure, then the best way to uphold the promise is through a written contract. Regardless of the outside forces, the intent of granting a gift will be enforced. Likewise, since many prosecuting angels who stand to interfere with our prayers on Rosh Hashana were created by our sins, Am Yisrael pleads with God to be inscribed in the book of life in order to thwart any cancellation of His promise. The prosecution's arguments will not hold since God committed in writing to grant us life. So, more than asking God to remember us for life, we equally pray that He inscribes us in the book of life. What is the best approach to seeing the fulfillment of this request?

It is God's wish to spoil with His infinite kindness all His created worlds and beings. God's natural inclination is to release an unrestrained

44 R. Levy Yitzhak of Berditchev, *Kedushat Levy* Rosh Hashana,

stream of abundance to a beneficiary. God delights in His Creation when mankind is the recipient of this goodness. But when man is undeserving, because of his deeds or lack of them, the divine flow of kindness cannot find a receiving end. Instead, it is captured by the *chitzonim*, the forces of evil. Their ranks are strengthened as they feed off God's blessings. The idea of *galut haShechinah*, the divine flow of abundance, is diverted to the forces of destruction. The impact of the latter's growth is manifest through international upheavals and wars whose intended first victims are invariably the Jewish communities, their synagogues and house of studies. Through these catastrophes, the *chitzonim*'s strength translates into uprooting *yeshivot* and weakening the spread of Torah.

Consequently, when we pray to God to grant us life and sustenance, it should be with the intent of being the receiving end of God's goodness, rather than of satisfying our material needs. In this manner, we meet God's design to bestow His kindness upon mankind, and we cause Him to delight in us. This way, the recipient becomes a donor, as he too grants God contentment. So, when we urge God to remember us for life, *zochrenu l'Chaim*, we ask Him to make of us a *zachar*, male donor, with God being the recipient of our delight.

The mystical idea of man acting as a provider to the Divine is equally highlighted in the prayer verses recited on Rosh Hashana where we assert God's Kingship over the world. As a Ruler, God commands the attribute of *Malchut*, kingship; He has the last say. Likewise, the righteous Jew is granted the power to void God's decrees. This corresponds to the *tzaddik's* authority over the attribute of *Malchut. Imru lefanai malchuyot* – proclaiming God's Kingship, equally reads as an invitation from God to Am Yisrael, to assert their attribute of *Malchut* by which they can cancel a divine decree. In this situation, God becomes the recipient of man's initiative, where man decrees and God executes. Consequently, the greatest liaison between God and the righteous is established.

Although Rosh Hashana is a day when man is judged, God accords the Jewish repentant the opportunity to inscribe himself in the book of life. Through his penitence and prayers, the Jewish individual can override, as it were, God's decree and replace it with a favorable outcome. One approach to achieving this result is by minimizing the *galut haShechinah*, that is, by benefiting from the divine abundance for the sake of God's glory, rather than for one's material gains. ■

The Sound of the Shofar Sets Off a Tikkun

According to the Arizal, on Rosh Hashana, the three series of *shofar* sounded affect a *tikkun* to the three cardinal sins. These are prohibited acts over which one must be willing to sacrifice his life, even under duress, rather than transgress them. The first segment is when the congregation is seated (*tekiot demiyushav*). It instigates a *tikkun* to the sin of idol worship. During the silent prayer, the *shofar* is blown a second time initiating a *tikkun* to the sin of illicit relations, and the final sequence sets off a *tikkun* to the spilling of blood.

The three *shofar* sounds equally correspond to the three glorifications we address to God on Rosh Hashana.[45] *Malchuyot*, the Kingship verses of praise, proclaim God as King of the universe and are an antithesis to idol worship. The second set of verses, *Zichronot*, highlights God's infinite power to recall all men's actions and to judge them. They atone for the sin of prohibited relations. These acts disregard God's omnipresence and deny the idea of *hashgacha pratit* – God's constant awareness of man's actions and thoughts. The *Zichronot* verses assert that there is no forgetfulness before the glorious Throne of God. Finally, *Shofarot* are the verses describing the formidable *shofar* sounds which accompanied God's descent on Mount Sinai. They also invoke the sound of the *shofar* that heralds the coming of the Mashiach. The *shofar* represents a *tikkun* to the spilling of blood because its sound is likened to the breath of life which God blew into Adam's nostrils. It is an antithesis to taking one's life.

Likewise, the three Patriarchs' unique approach in worshipping God affected a *tikkun* to these three sins. Idol worship is rectified by our forefather Isaac who was sacrificed upon the altar, a site commonly used by idol worshippers. Abraham dedicated his life to remedy the sin of forbidden relations. He carried the conduct of *tzniut,* modesty to such

45 *Shem MiShmuel*, Rosh Hashana 33

heights that he did not glance at his own wife.[46] As to Jacob, the Torah states that, during his life, he never saw wasted semen, the source of existence. Through this conduct, he performed a *tikkun* to the sin of spilling the innocents' blood.

Similarly, the Zohar adds that the three distinct sounds of the *shofar* – *Tekiah*, *Shevarim*, and *Teruah* – correspond to the saintly ways of life of Abraham, Isaac and Jacob. In the lengthy and turbulent road of exile, the spiritual influence of the three patriarchs stands by and protects the Jewish People from the three cardinal sins. It is in this merit that the Jewish People is accorded the same honor as the ministering angels, heralding God's holiness each day: "*Kadosh, Kadosh, Kadosh*" – "Holy! Holy! Holy is Hashem, Master of Hosts." One who is immersed in depraved immorality is undeserving of sanctifying God's name.

Furthermore, the Talmud discloses that on Rosh Hashana, Joseph was freed from jail and appointed viceroy of Egypt.[47] This historical event precisely took place on Rosh Hashana, the Day of Judgment, to reflect the character attributes of Joseph as conferred on him by his own name. It is known that the Hebrew name of an individual reveals the essence of his being. When our Matriarch Rachel gave birth to her son, she named him Yosef, which means to add, and prayed God give her another son. So Joseph's essence implies a thirst for continuous spiritual growth. In his worship of God, Joseph never reached a satisfying plateau, and sought to add more. Thus the idea of "*od Yosef chai*," identifying Joseph with life's uninterrupted renewal. Joseph was set free on Rosh Hashana because this day is equally defined by the necessity to increment our religious devotion. The essence of Rosh Hashana, which is similar to that of Joseph, provided a spiritual justification for freeing him on that day. Starting on Rosh Hashana, and for the subsequent ten days of penitence until Yom Kippur, we are required to increase our Torah observance and prayers and emulate Joseph's essence of gradual and constant growth in the worship of God. ■

---

46 Rashi on Genesis 12:11

47 BT *Rosh Hashana* 10b

Praying with Humility

The Midrash teaches that God showed Jacob in a dream the guardian angels of the four nations who would subjugate Israel later in history.[48] Jacob saw the angel of Babylon climbing and descending the ladder whose end reached the heavens. Then, he saw the angel of Persia going up and coming down, and the angels of Greece and finally Rome ascending the ladder's rungs, then descending. At that moment, God invited Jacob to climb up. Jacob realized that all these nations, who rose to power, suffered humiliating demise. As he feared a similar fate for his descendants, he refused to go up. God assured Jacob that if he climbs up the ladder now, he will never experience a downfall. Still, Jacob remained hesitant and refused to go up. On account of this absence of faith, and as a *tikkun*, God informed Jacob that his progeny will be exiled and subdued by the above four kingdoms. It is difficult to think that Yaakov Avinu, the forefather of Israel, would display such a lack of faith.[49]

Looking back at the rise of many empires, it was invariably followed by their fall. The root cause was the haughtiness these nations displayed following their triumphs.

Nebuchadnezzar, the emperor of Babylon claimed: "I will ascend over the tops of the clouds; I will liken myself to the Most High."[50]

Hiram, the king of Tyre said: "I am god; I occupy the seat of God in the heart of the seas!"[51]

Alluding to Edom's arrogance, God responds:[52] "Even if you raise your nest like an eagle or if you place your nest among the stars, I will bring you down from there."[53] The conceitedness of these nations is the cause of their decline.

48 *Vayikrah Rabbah* 29
49 *Shem MiShmuel*, Rosh Hashana 72
50 Isaiah 14:14
51 Ezekiel 28:2
52 Obadiah 1:4
53 Perhaps this is an allusion to the space stations.

On the other hand, it is Am Yisrael's nature to act with humility whenever they achieve greatness, as they remain aware of God's kindness and, mostly, that He owes them nothing. They inherited this character trait from their forefather Abraham who said of himself: "I am but dust and ash."[54] When he was invited to climb up to higher spheres, Jacob refused because he feared the trap of haughtiness. Jacob is also known as "*Ish Ohalim*," the man who dwells in the tents of Torah, the antithesis to haughtiness. God's invitation could conflict with Israel's natural inclination to run away from conceit.

Still, Jacob's refusal was viewed as disobedience to God's wish, for he should have rushed to act upon His command without personal considerations or calculations. At that moment, it was incumbent upon Jacob to void his reasoning and act with full faith in God. It was then decreed that Jacob's progeny would be subjugated by these four nations. The objective of these exiles will consist in repairing the failure of their forefather, by demonstrating unrelenting faith in God, notwithstanding the economic and military triumphs of these nations, and by voiding their personal concerns in this process.

The concluding words of this Midrash relay Jacob's agony when he heard God's decree:

"Could it be that the exile under Edom will be unending?"

God reassured him: "But as for you, do not be afraid, My servant, Jacob, and do not be frightened, O Israel, for behold, I am saving you from afar, and your offspring from the land of their captivity."[55]

On Rosh Hashana, as the Jews acknowledge God's Kingship over the world, they stand before Him with humility praying for a favorable outcome. Thanks to this character trait and to the sound of the *shofar*, the prosecuting angels are silenced and God walks away from His Throne of Justice to settle instead on the Throne of Compassion from where verdicts of mercy are released. So, in his final address to Israel, Moses

54 Genesis 18:27
55 Jeremiah 46:27

disclosed the reason God selected them as the Chosen People: "Not because you are more numerous than all the peoples did Hashem desire you and choose you, for you are the fewest of all the peoples."[56] Says Rashi: "You make yourselves the smallest." God would not contemplate an extraordinary relationship with any other nation except Israel because of Israel's meekness. Indeed, the Creator of the universe shows no tolerance for the haughty heart. ■

May the Year and Its Curses Come to an End!

The Talmud suggests that Ezra, who led the Jews back to the Land of Israel from Persia in the Jewish year 3408, arranged the weekly Torah reading in such a way that the chapters in Deuteronomy enunciating the fearful curses would always be read close to Rosh Hashana.[57] It is so, adds the Talmud, that the year and its curses would come to an end.

Rabbi Yehoshua of Belz explains that when reading these dreadful pending tribulations, a person will experience remorse over his misdeeds and embrace the path of repentance.[58] This reaction will be favorably viewed in heaven and it will be considered as if this individual has indeed suffered all those curses. Essentially, by reading the curses before year's end, and by acknowledging our transgressions, we issue our own sentence, as it were, thus taking away the case from the hands of the heavenly court. The latter will have no reason for passing unfavorable judgments against us.

A similar idea is introduced by the Talmud regarding sacrificial offerings.[59] Although we are not able to bring a sacrifice, it is treated in heaven as if we have performed this commandment just by studying its pertinent text in the Torah. Such is the concept taught by the Prophet "and let our lips substitute for bulls."[60] Since the Temple is not available to offer sacri-

56 Deuteronomy 7:7
57 BT *Megillah* 31b
58 R. Friedman, *Shvilei Pinchas*, Ki Tavo, 5768
59 BT *Menachot* 110a
60 Hosea 14:3

fices, we replace the act with Torah study and prayers. While in exile, the best tool for our individual *tikkun* rests with learning Torah.

Moreover, the Talmud teaches that all the curses in question were initiated by Moses[61] at the end of his life.[62] Unlike the first set of forty-nine curses found in Leviticus,[63] Moses's list numbers ninety-eight. What prompted Moses, the caring leader, to issue such threatening curses against Am Yisrael? Also, why did God deliver precisely forty-nine curses?

The Zohar[64] answers this question explaining that the Torah was given with forty-nine levels of holiness and forty-nine levels of impurity. A balance between the forces of good and evil must always be maintained as to accord man the ability to exercise his freedom of choice. Whenever a sinful act is committed, man falls into one or many of these forty-nine levels of contamination depending on the sin's gravity. The individual's soul will be defiled in proportion to the seriousness of his spiritual failure. Consequently, God issued forty-nine curses as atonement for the forty-nine facets of impurity.

At the same time, although one might entertain an evil thought, God discards it and does not count it as an actual evil deed. It is because man's thought sits within his soul, and when he contemplates a sinful thought he sullies the soul. As the latter represents a Godly portion, God, in His compassion, readily foregoes what is due to Him and ignores the sinful thought.[65] It is not treated as a sin. Yet, our Sages urge us to express remorse over the forbidden thoughts as much as over the actual transgressions.[66] As the sinful thoughts equally require full atonement, Moses released ninety-eight curses which would be read prior to Rosh Hashana and would act as atonement for the forty-nine levels of defilement generated by one's thoughts and forty-nine levels of impurity created by our sinful acts.

61 The Tosefot clarify that Moses wrote the curses though *Ruach HaKodesh* while the first set of curses in Bechukotai were dictated by Hashem to Moses.

62 BT *Megillah* 31b

63 Leviticus 25:14-43

64 Shemot 15b

65 *Chidah Ma'arechet* 5:8

66 BT *Yomah* 29a

In fact, one should not overlook the seriousness of a contemplated sin just because it was never realized. Our thoughts reflect our spirituality and are interchangeable with our identity. As such, our individual holiness is fully defined by the substance of our thoughts. Similarly, our schism with God will be driven by the vile nature of our thoughts. They will invariably drag us into the forty-nine levels of *tumah*. This is the reason our Sages strongly emphasize a repentance for improper thoughts.

The reading of these frightening curses at the close of the year should inspire us with awe and a surge for *teshuvah*. It would bring to an end the year and its curses. May the New Year and its blessings begin! ■

Yom Kippur

Yom Kippur

Rosh Hashana and Yom Kippur equally invoke God's kindness since Creation which took place on Rosh Hashana was itself an act of divine kindness. It is so because God brought man to this material world to earn a place in the Olam Habbah *in his own right. This reward will be the result of man's individual daily struggles, rather than of an external benevolent intervention. Just as God's absolute Oneness is independent of any external influence, so man's reward in* Olam Habbah *will only result from his own merit. This is true* chessed *of God, as man is given the opportunity to emulate his Creator by attaining his ultimate goal without any outside interference. God's kindness is reaffirmed during this period through His forgiveness as a response to our* teshuvah. *Although some of our sins are so severe that they leave in the upper worlds deeply entrenched blemishes that would require lengthy and complex process of repentance, the spiritual benefit of* Neilah *can remove these stains.*

Who Is Azazel?

Moses's prayers for obtaining forgiveness for the sin of the Golden Calf concluded on the tenth of Tishrei, the day he came back from Sinai with the second Tablets of the Law. That day became known as Yom Kippur, the day of forgiveness for generations to come.

Inside the Temple, the highlight of the day was the special service performed by the High Priest as related in the following lines: "From the assembly of the Children of Israel he shall take two he-goats for a sin offering and one ram for a burnt-offering... Aaron shall place lots upon the two he-goats: one lot for Hashem and one lot for *Azazel*... And the he-goat designated by lot for *Azazel* shall be stood alive before Hashem, to provide atonement through it, to send it to *Azazel* to the Wilderness."[1]

Who is *Azazel*?[2] What does he stand for and why must these two he-goats be of equal height, equal monetary value and physical resemblance?[3]

Our Sages explain that life's challenges are proportional to one's spiritual stature.[4] The higher the spirituality of a person, the higher will be his temptations. It is so, because God has established that the essence of life rests with man's ability to choose between good and evil. To this end, it becomes imperative that the tendency to do good be equal to the inclination toward evil. Otherwise, short of this balance, a person will be deprived of his faculty of choice, as the predominant force will invariably gain the upper hand. To this end, the Hebrew word *Azazel* recalls this concept through its acronym which stands for "God has created these opposing forces to counter each other, עזאזל = זה לעמות זה עשה א-לוקים, *Azazel = zeh le umat zeh assah Elokim.*"[5]

The true significance of man is defined by his personal motivation, otherwise known as the good or evil inclination.[6] Man's heart can lean toward

1 Leviticus 16:5
2 R. Friedman, *Shvilei Pinchas*, Elul 2008
3 BT *Yomah* 62a
4 BT *Sukkah* 52a
5 Mahari Mi'Kamarna, Bechukotai 295
6 R. Tzaddok HaKohen of Lublin, *Tzidkat Tzaddik* 248

noble traits or malevolent behavior. This is the true meaning of "*zeh le umat zeh assah Elokim.*" God has created, within each individual, opposing forces of comparable influence to counter each other. The greatness of an individual reveals an equal amount of evil which he subdued through personal effort.

Likewise, man's specific character weakness is a clear indication of his potential for greatness. If one is led by his desires to satisfy certain immoral pursuits, he should know that, there is within himself, as much goodness to reverse his destructive cravings.

So when the Torah requires that these two he-goats must be of equal height, equal monetary value and physical resemblance, it is because God wants us to be aware of our potential for *teshuvah* on Yom Kippur.[7] Both the forces of good and evil are always equal, and man should not fear the upcoming struggle. Any form of spiritual failure represents the strongest evidence of the spiritual capabilities which are sitting in one's heart and are simply waiting to be utilized.

With this introduction, we can attempt to better understand the role of *Azazel* on Yom Kippur: "And the he-goat designated by lot for *Azazel* shall be stood alive before Hashem, to provide atonement through it, to send it to *Azazel* to the Wilderness." How does this procedure – at the end of which the red ribbon attached around the animal's horn, miraculously turns white – clean the sins of Am Yisrael?

Since *Azazel* identifies the Evil Inclination, Am Yisrael acknowledges the demarcation between two separate camps which define the created world.[8] These are the world of Torah and the world of evil. Esau is identified by what he values best: "By your sword you shall live."[9] It is his essence and enjoyment. Each month, children and adults watch countless murder scenes on TV. Yet, no one is repulsed because it is a source of entertainment.

On the other hand, Am Yisrael belongs to the camp of Torah as in: "The voice [of Torah] is Jacob's voice."[10] This constitutes our *nachat*, a ful-

7 BT *Yomah* 62a

8 *Sichot HaGrash Pincus*, Elul 380

9 Genesis 27:40

10 Ibid., 27:22

fillment of life's true objective. As long as each side keeps to its camp, then there is no conflict, and *Azazel* is content with its lot, the he-goat. Conflict arises only when two people want the same thing. When Am Yisrael unequivocally recognizes its own camp, the camp of Torah, and when it acknowledges that it has nothing to do with the other camp, the *goyish* culture (the foreign culture), than that is the best manifestation of *teshuvah*.

The Rambam writes that through the he-goat that is sent to *Azazel*, all the sins of an individual – whether they were committed intentionally or unintentionally, whether he knew of them or was unaware of them – are forgiven providing that the person adopts a path of repentance.[11] On Yom Kippur, the repentance is less on adhering to the prohibited and the permitted, and more on identifying one's ideological camp. It is the camp of the fear of God and of *emunat hachamim*, belief in the teachings of our Sages. These two traditional paths lead to genuine *teshuvah*. ■

NEILAH: THE HEIGHT OF YOM KIPPUR

A story is told about a childless couple from Zidon who visited Rabbi Shimon bar Yochai. They explained that they cared a great deal for each other but they had to separate as they could not bring children after ten years of marriage. The Rabbi suggested that they should celebrate their separation in the same way they celebrated their union. The couple followed the Rabbi's advice and they had a festive dinner. Then, the husband who had consumed a few drinks, asked his wife to take from the house whatever she desires most before returning to her parents. After he fell asleep, she had her servants carry him over to her parents' home. When he sobered-up, he turned to his wife and asked what was he doing at his in-laws? "Did you not ask me to take what I most desire from your home? I desire nothing more in the world than you!" They both went back to Rabbi Shimon bar Yochai and told him the story. He was so moved by the purity of their intentions that he gave them a blessing and she soon bore a child.

During *Neilah*, God is telling us: "Open wide your mouth and I will fill it."[12] Ask what you wish of me! An intelligent person should "grab the

11 *Laws of Teshuvah*, 1:2

12 Psalms 81:11

husband" and cry out: "Master of the Universe! It is You that I want and nothing else!" Through this closeness to God, we will merit all the *yeshuot* and *rachamim*, divine salvations and compassion.

The pinnacle of Yom Kippur, the Day of Atonement, is *Neilah*. This is a time when a Jew can achieve through prayer what he cannot accomplish during the entire year.[13] It is at this moment of the day, that all the *Sefirot* of the created worlds experience an elevation uniting them to the *Keter*, the highest *Sefirah*.[14] It is the propitious time to beseech the Cre-

13 *Sichot HaGrash Pincus*, Elul 412

14 The masters of mystical teachings reveal that all created worlds emanate from the ten *Sefirot*, the attributes of Creation: *Keter, Chochmah, Binah, Chessed, Gevurah, Tiferet, Netzach, Hod, Yesod,* and *Malchut*. These ten attributes maintain interdependency with one another in the same way a flame is attached to its supporting braze of fire. Notwithstanding this internal relationship, each attribute maintains a separate link directly with its common Source, the *Ein Sof*, the Infinite Wisdom, blessed be He. Through this direct connection, every attribute unites all the created worlds to their Creator. This unity causes God's bounty to flow from the upper to the lower worlds.

The ten *Sefirot* correspond to the Tetragrammaton, *Yud keh vav keh*. The first and second letters of God's name, yud and hei, are linked to three *Sefirot*: *Keter*, Crown, which defines purpose, to the *Sefirah* of *Chochmah*, Wisdom, and to the *Sefirah* of *Binah*, Understanding, which relates to logic. The third letter, *vav*, is identified with the next six *Sefirot: Chessed, Gevurah, Tiferet, Netzach, Hod,* and *Yesod,* which translate respectively as Loving-kindness, Strength, Beauty, Dominance, Splendor, and Foundation. The last letter, *hei*, corresponds to the *Sefirah* of *Malchut*, Kingship.

The Creator is known as *Ein Sof*, Infinite One. We must never associate Him with any shape, form, or image in our imagination because such association will imply physical limitation, God forbid. For the benefit of man, God created five upper worlds known as *Adam Kadmon, Atzilut, Beriah, Yetzirah,* and *Asiyah*. The four lower universes – Emanation, Creation, Formation and Completion – correspond to the four letters of the Tetragrammaton, *Yud keh vav keh*. The universe of *Adam Kadmon* corresponds to the apex of the *yud*, from the first letter of God's name. *Adam Kadmon*, the highest universe and closest to the *Ein Sof*, is passed over in our discussions because it is completely hidden. This is also the reason *Adam Kadmon* corresponds to the apex of the *yud* only and not to a full letter. The fundamental structure of these five worlds is comprised of God's name, corresponding to the four elements — water, wind, fire, and earth — and to the ten *Sefirot* (*yud* equals 10). This structure propagates itself to the smallest particle on

ator to grant us our needs. In fact, the Ramchal goes further in suggesting that, at this moment, one has the potential of reaching the spiritual status of Adam prior to his sin.

Rosh Hashana and Yom Kippur equally invoke God's kindness since Creation which took place on Rosh Hashana, was itself an act of divine kindness. It is so because God brought man to this material world to earn a place in the *Olam Habbah* in his own right. This reward will be the result of man's individual daily struggles, rather than of an external benevolent intervention. Just as God's absolute Oneness is independent of any external influence, so man's reward in *Olam Habbah* will only result from his own merit. This is true *chessed* of God, as man is given the opportunity to emulate his Creator by attaining his ultimate goal without any outside interference.

Likewise, God's kindness is reaffirmed on Yom Kippur through His forgiveness as a response to our *teshuvah*. Although some of our sins are so severe that they leave in the upper worlds deeply entrenched blemishes that would require lengthy and complex process of repentance, the spiritual benefit of *Neilah* can remove these stains. In a manifestation of unrestrained divine kindness, God offered Am Yisrael this period of spiritual renewal in exchange for their commitment to abandoning a way of life which is contrary to Torah.

The question remains: how is one able to reach the spiritual zenith that the Ramchal is talking about?

The Chafetz Chaim tells the story of a prince who was exiled by the king to a far away city. As many years passed, the king arrived to this

---

earth — no entity within creation can exist were it not for the detailed, albeit reduced, presence of the divine name and the ten *Sefirot* within that element. The ten *Sefirot* constitute the internal structure of each universe and reflect a filtering process of God's awesome light in the same way each one of the above worlds does. This fascinating process of diminishing God's light is for the benefit of man, who is expected to exercise his free will to uncover God in the midst of divine concealment within our physical world (R. Chaim Vital, *Da'at U'Tevunah*, 24; *Sha'arei Kedushah*).

distant land and received, among other dignitaries, his son. The latter eloquently begged his father that a specific amount of money be sent to him yearly to meet his expenses. The king replied: "You are a silly young man; you should ask that I bring you home and all your needs will be satisfied."

During *Neilah*, we should focus less on our personal needs and more on the exile of the *Shechinah*, the Divine Presence.[15] We should direct our prayers during these precious moments toward the rebuilding of the Holy Temple, the return of the *Shechinah* to Jerusalem, the renewal of the services by the High Priest, the Kohanim and the Levites. Then, all of God's blessings will automatically flow upon us and the world. When man prays for his health and financial stability, he draws God's blessings only upon his household. But when his wish is to see God's Glory descend upon the earth, all of creation benefits from this prayer.

Granted, we might not attain the spiritual level of Adam before he sinned or cause the Divine Presence to descend upon Jerusalem, as yet, but there is no doubt, says the Ramchal, that, during *Neilah*, our *tefillah* will effect a gradual *tikkun* in the upper worlds which ultimately will produce the desired results.

The effect of Yom Kippur corresponds to King David's words: "I am Hashem, your God, who raised you from the land of Egypt; open wide your mouth and I will fill it."[16] On this day, God is asking that we submit our requests without restraint. The day itself has a built-in power to purify us: "For on this day he shall provide atonement for you to cleanse you; from all your sins…"[17] As God's kindness permeates Yom Kippur, we should rise to the occasion and optimize this unparalleled opportunity to pray for a more spiritual world as well as for our ultimate benefit. ■

---

15 Man's sins cause the fall of the Divine Presence and push it away from God, its Source. (The Divine Presence is the manifestation of God in this world.) Through the performance of the mitzvot and prayer, we elevate the *Shechinah* and close the schism that separates it from its Source. This action triggers the flow of heavenly blessings upon the world.

16 Psalms 81:11

17 Leviticus 16:30

Considerate Behavior with Each Other

The Talmud tells the story of Rav Rechumei who always returned home from yeshiva on the eve of Yom Kippur to be with his wife.[18] The yeshiva was under the leadership of the great scholar Ravah. It was located in the city of Mechuza in Babylon. It was customary then for young married students to leave their wives for a long period of time to study Torah. One time, Rav Rechumei was so much involved in his learning that he missed the caravan that would take him home for Yom Kippur. Meanwhile, his wife who eagerly awaited her husband's arrival realized that he would not be with her on Yom Kippur. She felt deeply disappointed and her eyes filled with tears. At that very moment, continues the Talmud, Rav Rechumei who was still in Mechuza, fell and died. It was, suggests the Talmud, a divine retribution for causing grief to his wife.

Rav Rechumei did not intend any harm to his wife. Yet, since he caused her chagrin, he was punished. Moreover, we can imagine her inconsolable sorrow when she heard the tragic news that she would never see her husband again. This story highlights the severity of hurting someone's feelings.[19] The consequences are unrelated to divine intervention. Rather, it is the built-in nature of an insensitive behavior. Whoever is not careful with his fellow man's sensitivity is likened to stepping into a fire. Regardless of the intent, he will still burn.

The Maharal explains that the concept of strife came into existence on the second day of Creation along with *Gehinnom*, a place where the sinners' souls expiate their disregard of the divine commandments through suffering.[20] Whoever gets involved in a dispute, will invariably draw upon him or her, the perilous influence of *Gehinnom*, regardless of that person's merits or intention.

Thus in a discussion on the impressive effects of Yom Kippur, Rabbi Elazar ben Azaria teaches that it only causes the cleansing of the transgressions which man commits toward His Creator, but Yom Kippur does

18 BT *Ketubot* 62b

19 R. Chaim Shmuelevitz, *Sichot Mussar* 105,

20 Maharal, *Gur Aryeh* on Korach

not help with the unkind attitude shown to others.[21] First, one must ask for and obtain forgiveness from his fellow man before Yom Kippur.

Even if a person displays an inappropriate attitude for a noble reason, he will not escape the harsh consequences built in the hurt he causes others. Peninnah, the wife of Elkanah, lost her children because she mercilessly taunted the childless Hannah.[22] The Talmud suggests that Peninnah's intention was pure.[23] It was to create an incentive for Hannah to plead with God to bless her with children. Still, Peninnah suffered the consequences of her insensitive words to Hannah. Here too, we see the manifestation of the damages built in an unkind conduct. These outcomes do not represent a divine punishment. Rather, they are a natural end result to a wrongful behavior with our fellow man.

Commenting on the wise words of King Solomon: "One who is not good will punish even the righteous,"[24] Rabbi Yaakov teaches that whoever is in any way involved in the suffering to his fellowman, will never be allowed into the divine partition when he leaves this world.[25,26]

As a supporting argument, Rabbi Yaakov relates the dramatic events which brought about the death of King Ahab.[27] In order to acquire Naboth's vineyard, King Ahab and his wife Jezebel had him falsely accused of blasphemy and put to death. Then, the prophet Micaiah – who had received an extraordinary vision – informed King Ahab that Naboth's spirit had volunteered to return to earth for the purpose of misleading King Ahab and inciting him to go to war against Aram where he would meet his end. Although Naboth's spirit carried God's wish, his soul was not allowed back into the glorious divine partition which it once occupied. The Talmud learns this remarkable fact from God's reply to Naboth's offer:

21 BT *Yomah* 85b
22 I Samuel 1:2
23 BT *Bava Batra* 16a
24 Proverbs 17:26
25 BT *Shabbat* 149b
26 This is one of the reasons we recite the "Shema" at bed time along with other verses proclaiming our readiness to forgive those who wronged us in any manner.
27 I Kings 22:21

"And Hashem said, 'You will lure him and you will succeed! Go forth and do so!'"[28] Asks the Talmud: "what is the meaning of go forth?" Since it seems superfluous, the Talmud answers: "Leave My partition." Naboth's spirit was not seeking revenge. Rather, he wanted to sanctify God's Name by showing the people that King Ahab's crime will not go unpunished. Naboth's soul was willing to be taken away from the Divine Presence for the sanctity of God's Name.

Notwithstanding Naboth's lofty intent, his soul did not regain its earlier high status since he was involved in the death of King Ahab. Although Naboth carried out God's command, he still suffered because he was a stumbling block to a fellow man. Such is the unforgiving nature of a hurtful act or word against someone, which renders the need to seek forgiveness before Yom Kippur more pressing.

As this alarming lesson deals with hurtful conduct, and presents its grave consequences, we can learn the benefits of the opposing behavior – when man acts with kindness, for God's attribute of compassion is immensely superior to that of retribution.[29] One who stands behind the material advancement, and most importantly, the spiritual growth of his friend will undoubtedly deserve to dwell within God's *mehitza*, partition. ■

For the Good of the Community

When Jonah received the divine message to travel to Nineveh and to warn its inhabitants, he ran away from his mission fearing that it would bring shame upon the Jewish People.[30] Jonah reasoned that in Nineveh, the gentiles would hear his message and repent, as indeed they did, while the Jews in Israel were ignoring the prophets' exhortations. This contradiction between the gentiles' behavior and the Jews' conduct would strengthen the prosecution against Israel in heaven.[31]

---

28 Ibid., 22:22

29 Rashi, Exodus 34:7: "God's attribute of kindness is five hundred times greater than His attribute of justice."

30 Rav Chaim Shmuelevitz, *Sichot Mussar* 94

31 *Midrash Tanchumah*, Vayikrah 8

Jonah was not worried about transgressing the Torah commandment prohibiting a prophet from withholding his prophecy. A divine revelation through prophecy is only possible in the Holy Land.[32] When Jonah left the boundaries of the Land of Israel he was no longer fit to receive a divine message. He caught a boat heading for Tarshish outside the Land of Israel. For the sake of sparing Israel from an implied condemnation, Jonah was willing to lose his spiritual status as a prophet.

Following a mighty tempest, the sailors, who feared for their lives and who had linked the raging storm to God's displeasure with their passenger, threw Jonah into the sea. God designated a large fish to swallow Jonah and he remained in the fish's innards for three days and three nights. Undoubtedly, Jonah suffered during these three days without food or drink. Still, he did not pray, as he would rather die than come out to safety and carry out a mission that embarrasses the people of Israel. However, when the male fish threw him out and he was swallowed by a female large fish, Jonah could not bear remaining within its innards.[33] The discomfort was just too agonizing. It is only then, that he started praying and was saved.

Jonah's self-sacrifice on behalf of Israel was so dear to God that He did not select a different prophet to carry the message to Nineveh. Since he cared for Israel's honor, Jonah was elevated to higher spiritual levels and deserved to live through so many divine miracles. If one can gain so much by eliminating a prosecuting voice against the Jewish People, how much more would a person achieve when he or she creates for others opportunities to study Torah and accomplish deeds of kindness?

Similarly, Hanania, Mishael and Azaria were called by King Nebuchadnezzar of Babylon to attend his idol inauguration ceremony and to prostrate to the idol.[34] They could have run away. Instead, they showed up at the well-attended event and refused to bow before the idol, well aware that the King would put them to death. Nebuchadnezzar threw

---

32 Rashi, Jonah 1:3

33 Jonah 2:1-2. When referring to the large fish, the Bible alternates from the male to the female, indicating that he was swallowed twice.

34 BT *Sanhedrin* 92b

them into a fiery furnace, but God saved them. When they came out in the presence of the world's diplomatic corps, there was a great *Kiddush Hashem*, a sanctification of God's name. On that day, all the *goyim* shattered their idols. Hanania, Mishael and Azaria wanted to humiliate and lower idol worshipping in the eyes of their exiled brethrens. They sought to call the attention of the exiled Jews to the dangers of assimilation. They were ready to sacrifice their lives to spread this message to their community.

The Torah holds in high esteem those who teach the ways of God to members of the community: "And those who teach righteousness to the multitudes will shine like the stars, forever and ever."[35]

In a related discussion, Rabbi Meir Baal HaNess asks rhetorically: "Since God loves the poor people, why does He not provide for them?" To which he answers: "So that we will be saved from the harsh judgment of *Gehinnom* through the charity we give them."[36] Does this explanation make any sense? Is it acceptable for a poor man to suffer all his life so that rich people will be spared the torment of *Gehinnom*? It must be that the Torah views the necessity to save the multitudes from *Gehinnom* such a worthy cause for the poor that he should lead a life of needs and restrictions. In this regard, the good he does for the community is as great as what Hanania, Mishael and Azaria accomplished through their sacrifice. It is as precious as Jonah's *mesirut nefesh* for Israel.

During the afternoon service on Yom Kippur, we read the book of Jonah. Since Yom Kippur is a day of repentance and atonement, we evoke the repentance of the king of Nineveh and its inhabitants who abandoned their wicked ways when they heard Jonah's prophecy announcing the imminent destruction of their city. "And God saw their deeds that they repented from their evil way; and God relented concerning the evil He had said He would bring upon them, and did not do it."[37] God's compassion is invariably triggered by our *teshuvah* and observance of *mitzvot*. Of equal importance is our thoughtfulness toward our community. ■

35 Daniel 12:3

36 BT *Bava Batrah* 10a

37 Jonah 3:10

COMPLETING THE NESHAMA'S TASK

Our Sages teach that when a man accomplishes a good deed or fulfills one mitzvah, and at that moment God is judging the world and deciding its fate, then the balance is tilted in favor of the world thanks to that mitzvah.[38] How is it possible for a single individual to save the entire world through one action? In order to shed some light on this remarkable concept, we must look back at the spiritual status of the world when only Adam lived.

Our Sages teach that all the *neshamot* of Am Yisrael are connected to each other with a strong bond.[39] When the world was created, all these souls were rooted within various limbs of *Adam HaRishon*. Had he not sinned, he would have achieved the world's *tikkun* in unison with all these *neshamot*. As a result of Adam's sin, all these *neshamot* fell away in a process known as "*shevirah*" – the scattering of the souls. These holy souls were then confined in inanimate objects, in the plant life, and in the animal world. As a result of Adam's *teshuvah*, many souls – albeit not all – were redeemed and saved in a heavenly chamber called "*heichal haneshamot*" from where they descend into a human body for further *tikkunim* through life.

Subsequently, it became man's mission to rectify the original spiritual harm by redeeming all the scattered souls and elevating them to their Divine Source. This task can be achieved only through the observance of the Torah commandments.

Additionally, when one succeeds in serving God with all the components of his soul – *nefesh*, *ruach*, *neshama*, and *yechidah* – he triggers a *teshuvah* movement among all the individuals whose *neshamot* share the same root as his own. By the same token, all the scattered souls which belong to the parent *neshama* are uplifted. Until these holy souls are redeemed from their fall and reunited with their original root, the *neshama* must return to this world in a reincarnation to complete its task. This concept is illustrated by the Talmudic teaching: "One should not

38 BT *Kiddushin* 40b

39 *Maor Vashemesh,* Acharei Mot

appoint a leader of a community, unless he carries a basket of reptiles on his back."[40] The *neshama* of a Jewish leader may not be an accomplished soul. It must have its own shortcomings which the leader must correct at the same time that he uplifts the members of his community through his spiritual endeavor. He must relate to the numerous holy souls which fell during the *shevirah* process and which this Torah leader is able to redeem thanks to his *mitzvot*. At the same time, the Jewish leader can cause those individuals with the same *neshama* root as his to return to God's ways.

But if one's soul has no related holy *neshamot* scattered in various forms of life, then this individual cannot be in charge of the public's needs. He will not live long because a man in this situation can achieve the *tikkun* his soul requires in a relatively short time. The *neshamot* of Nadav and Avihu, the sons of Aaron, originated from a higher spiritual Source. No fallen holy souls were related to them. Their respective *tikkun* was brief; hence, they did not live long.

This clarifies the earlier mentioned teaching, that one who observes a divine commandment can favorably influence the outcome of the world. Through the performance of a mitzvah, one uplifts the fallen souls and causes many to return to God, which results in a positive judgment for the world. The *neshama* of Aaron, the High Priest, identified with a multitude of holy *neshamot*. Through his lofty service in the Sanctuary, he elevated many souls and helped others to come closer to God.

Aaron, however, was unable to impact the sinners to do *teshuvah* if they failed to show remorse. Hence, the divine injunction, "Speak to Aaron, he shall not come at all times into the Sanctuary."[41] In other words, he must not attempt to bring back to God those who obstinately resist *teshuvah*. Rather, Aaron's spiritual efforts helped only those who seek to repent. Such was the case throughout the year. But on Yom Kippur, a day on which even the wicked feel an awakening for *teshuvah*, then Aaron entered the *Kodesh HaKodashim*, Holy of Holies, to assist those *neshamot* which are distant from God, to return to their Creator.

---

40 BT *Yomah* 22b

41 Leviticus 16:1–3

The greatest period for the world's *tikkun* was in the times of Beit Hamikdash. On account of its holiness, it acted as an *even sho'evet*, a spiritual magnet on souls scattered throughout the world.[42] Since the destruction of Beit Hamikdash, the Jews had to go into exile to perform their *tikkun* in various lands where, at first, they were welcomed, and then kicked out by their host country once their *tikkun* in that specific land was completed. This last idea is alluded at by Jacob's address to his wives Rachel and Leah before leaving Haran: "and he said to them, 'I have noticed that your father's [Laban] disposition is not toward me as in earlier days.'"[43] As Jacob had finished elevating the souls scattered in Haran, he is ready to move on. Likewise, thanks to their prayers and Torah study, Jews continue the *tikkun* process to benefit the world wherever they are. ■

Seven Days for Seven Attributes

The Talmud relates that seven days prior to Yom Kippur, the Sages would separate the High Priest from his wife and move him to a chamber within the Temple.[44] During these days, they would review with him all the complicated rituals required on that holy day. These seven days correspond to the following seven attributes by which God administers His world:[45] Loving-kindness,[46] strength, pride, dominance, splendor, foundation, and Kingship.[47]

Since the role of the High Priest on Yom Kippur consists in obtaining atonement on behalf of the Jewish People, he must first highlight the weaknesses of Israel in an effort to rectify their shortcomings which are identified with those seven attributes. Each time a Jew transgresses a divine commandment, he causes a deep schism between his soul and his

---

42 R. Gedaliah Halevy Sherer, *Ohr Gedaliah* Jerusalem: 1990, on Shemini Atzeret quoting Ohr HaChaim and the Arizal

43 Genesis 31:5

44 Mishna *Yomah* 1:1

45 R. Levy Yitzhak of Berditchev, *Kedushat Levy, Perisha LeKohen Gadol,*

46 *Chessed, Gevurah, Tiferet, Netzach, Hod, Yesod, and Malchut* which translate respectively as Loving-kindness, Strength, Beauty, Dominance, Splendor, Foundation and Kingship

47 See p. 96 for additional comments about the ten *Sefirot*

Creator. This divide is restored by the prayers of the High Priest as well as by the holiness of Yom Kippur. It is equally repaired by the meditations of the High Priest inside the Holy of Holies, a once in a year occurrence. Last but not least, the atonement is provided by God's promise: "For on this day He shall provide atonement for you to cleanse you; from all your sins before Hashem shall you be cleansed."

On the first of the seven days of separation, the High Priest performs a *tikkun* for the attribute of *Chessed*, loving-kindness. Man's greatness is defined as worshipping God with love. Man fails when he redirects all his love to himself. Thanks to kindness, man can emulate his Creator and achieve greatness for others as well as for him. On the other hand, selfish motivation leads to destruction. It is the High Priest's function to amend this failing on behalf of Israel prior to Yom Kippur.

Similarly, the attribute of *Gevurah*, strength, translates into worshipping God with fear. It behooves man to remain constantly aware of God's presence everywhere and to tremble at the idea of disregarding His wishes. Without God's fear, one cannot possibly abide by His commandments. On the second day, the High Priest rectifies the failures associated with this attribute.

Also, in serving God, we should focus on making Him proud of us. This is achieved through *Tiferet*, sincere devotion. We must strive toward the realization of the prophet's words: "He said to me: 'You are My servant, Israel, in whom I take glory.'"[48] Rightly, honor and pride belong to God. These attributes do not agree with the haughty heart. It is the High Priest's responsibility to remedy this failure. This is accomplished on the third day.

On the fourth day of separation, the High Priest corrects the damage done to the attribute of *Netzach, d*ominance. It calls on man's struggle to win over the evil inclination. The perpetual fight between good and evil must be overcome. This attribute is damaged when man's life is regulated by his bad *yetzer*. As gratitude is the most essential requisite to worshipping God, man's challenge is to remain grateful to God despite the ma-

48 Isaiah 49:3

terialistic temptations. Through steadfast gratitude, man will be able to overcome his *yetzer*.

Likewise, on the fifth day, the High Priest will aim at rectifying any spiritual defect caused throughout the year to the attribute of *Hod*, splendor. This occurs when man takes credit for his material and spiritual successes and fails to give praise to the Creator for his accomplishment.

The attribute of *Yesod*, foundation, points at the connection which exists between man and God. It is breached when the rules governing this attribute are not maintained. *Yesod* regulates the laws pertaining to family purity and prohibited relations. When man is mostly dedicated to satisfying his physical desires, he forces an estrangement between God and himself. Ever since the Sages of the Great Assembly eliminated the *yetzer* for idol worship, the remnant forces of evil are concentrated on the attribute of *Yesod*, seeking man's downfall through illicit physical pursuits.[49] No other sinful conduct pushes God away from man as much as this failing. On the sixth day, the High Priest strives to repair the split between God and Israel.

On the seventh day, the High Priest consecrates his *tikkun* to the attribute of *Malchut*. Kingship deserves its rightful place; it only belongs to God: "Yours, Hashem, is the kingdom and the sovereignty over every leader."[50] In his unending material ambitions and pursuits, man fails to recognize this sobering fact.

The seven days of separation represent an opportunity for spiritual renewal for the High Priest. As he detaches himself from all forms of material life, he contemplates his worship of God under a different light. During these seven days which correspond to the seventy years of life, a new reality settles in. It is that God breathes life into every being, every moment of the day. Creation is constantly revitalized and this awareness causes a surge of spiritual anticipation which helps him accomplish the necessary *tikkun* for the seven attributes. The High Priest concludes that the best of man's emotions, be it love or reverence, pride or dominance,

49 BT *Yomah* 69b
50 I Chronicles 29:11

must be consecrated to God. Thus, on Yom Kippur itself, at the peak of the *tikkun* which results in the forgiveness of Am Yisrael's sins, the High Priest recalls the seven attributes while sprinkling the altar. They are verbally enunciated in this sequence: *achat ve'achat, achat ve'shtayim, achat ve'shalosh,* one and one, one and two, one and three, etc., where *achat* recalls the Oneness of God with which the accompanying attribute is uplifted. ■

Becoming the Person that God Envisioned

Each one of the commands issued to create the world concluded with a divine statement of approval: "*vayar Elokim ki tov*" – "and God saw that it was good." However, the tenth command, by which God created man, is short of this statement of satisfaction: "So God created man in His image, in the image of God He created him, male and female He created them."[51] Although man represents Creation's main objective, he seems to lack the perfection inherent in all other created items.[52] All were faultless – the stars, the plants, the animals, the mountains and the oceans. All were faultless – except for man.

Since man is imbued with the faculty of choice, he can act in the vilest fashion by following his animalistic instincts, thus bringing utter destruction to himself and his surroundings. This is the reason God refrained from praising His work. How could He extol the outcome of His handiwork knowing that man is capable of cruelty, selfishness, haughtiness and hatred? At the same time, man possesses the ability to rise to the highest spheres of moral behavior which would make God proud of His product. This explains why the tenth command is issued in the plural form: "Let us make Man." It is an invitation to man to partner with God in the making of man. Essentially, God is inviting man to participate in the task of creating himself. "Let us, you and I, make the man I envision." He will shine with greatness, nobility, generous heart, kindness, love and magnanimity. He will shy away from vindictiveness and callousness.

51 Genesis 1:27
52 Yismach Moshe, Genesis 1:26

And so, Yom Kippur, the last day of the Ten Days of Repentance, corresponds to the tenth command issued to create the world. On this day, our role is to evolve into the man which God envisioned.[53] It remains our duty to give *nachat*, pride to God through our individual, as well as, collective behavior.

Likewise, Rosh Hashana, the first day of the Ten Days of Repentance, corresponds to the first command God issued to create the world. What was that first command? "*Bereshit*, in the beginning of God's creating the heavens and the earth."[54] Rashi says on this verse: "On account of the people of Israel, who are called *Reshit*,[55] and on account of the Torah, who is also called *Reshit*,[56] God created the world." Israel and the Torah are the object of Creation. It is only through the Torah observance that Israel can rise to the highest spiritual levels and grant God, as it were, full justification for creating the world.

So, when a Jew utilizes the resources present in the world to promote Godliness, he adds vitality to the ten commands God had issued to create the world. These commands were never lost to space or time. They remain suspended in the heavens forever injecting a constant force of renewal into the world. King David praises God: "Forever, Hashem, Your word stands firm in the heavens."[57] In fact, this line is read out loud by the congregants on Rosh Hashana prior to taking out the Torah scroll.

But when man uses the world's resources to enhance his materialistic pursuits and to satisfy his greed, he weakens God's objective and impedes the blessings which are to uninterruptedly descend upon Creation from the ten commands issued to create the world.

The Mishna in *Avot* (5:1) describes the above scenario in the following words: "With ten utterances the world was created. What does

---

53 R. Friedman, *Shvilei Pinchas*, Rosh Hashana 5771

54 Genesis 1:1

55 Jeremiah 2:3 "Israel is holy to Hashem, the first [*reshit*] of His crop; all who devour it will be held guilty; evil shall come upon them – the word of Hashem"

56 Proverbs 8:22 "Hashem acquired me [the Torah] at the beginning [*reshit*] of His way."

57 Psalms 119:89

this come to teach us? Indeed, could it not have been created with one utterance? This was to exact punishment from the wicked who destroy the world that was created with ten utterances, and to bestow godly reward upon the righteous who sustain the world that was created by ten utterances." During the Ten Days of Repentance, every Jew is offered the opportunity to apply himself and rectify the spiritual damage he has caused these divine utterances. The height of this *tikkun* is on Rosh Hashana and on Yom Kippur. ■

Sukkot

Sukkot

R*abbeinu Bechai explains that the four species –* lulav, etrog, hadas *and* aravah *– correspond to the kingdoms of Babylon, Persia, Greece and Rome.*[1] *Throughout history, Israel was exiled and subjugated by these four nations. At the same time, the Maharal suggests that these four kingdoms symbolize the evil forces which drive idol worship, illicit relations, spilling of blood and* lashon hara *(evil speech). The latter, being as consequential in severity as the first three put together. The merit of the four species will keep in check the evil promoted by these nations. That is why Israel is given this commandment: "You shall take for yourselves on the first day the fruit of the citron tree, the branches of date palms, myrtle twigs, and brook willows; and you shall rejoice before Hashem, your God, for a seven-day period."*[2]

---

1 *Shem MiShmuel*, Sukkot 179

2 Leviticus 23:40

Gog and Magog Worship God to Attack Israel

"Why do nations gather, and regimes talk in vain? The kings of the earth take their stand and the princes conspire secretly, against Hashem and against His anointed."[3]

According to the Midrash in *Shocher Tov*, Pslams 2, these disturbing words represent a prelude to the Messianic Era when the forces of evil embodied by Gog and Magog will turn their devastating power against Israel.[4]

King David prophesized these dreadful threats along with a divine promise to shelter Israel and confound their enemies. Expounding on this prophecy, this Midrash reveals the nature of the nations' conspiracy:

"Cain was a fool," claims Esau, "he killed his brother Abel, while his father Adam was still bringing more children! I would be smarter: when the days of mourning for my father draw near, then I will kill my brother Yaakov."[5]

On the other hand, Pharaoh claims that Esau was a fool. "Did he not know that while he is waiting for his father's death, Jacob is multiplying? I would do better than that." Pharaoh commands his entire people, saying, "Every son that will be born – into the river shall you throw him!"[6]

Later in history, Haman labels Pharaoh a fool: "I shall not drown their first born. Rather, my edict will be 'to destroy, to slay and to exterminate all the Jews, from young to old, children and women, in one day.'"[7]

In the Messianic Times, however, Gog and Magog will ridicule the approach of Israel's early archenemies. "Don't they all know that Israel

3 Psalms 2:1
4 R. Yehudah L. Hossman, *Ohr Yahel*, Emor
5 Genesis 27:41
6 Exodus 1:22
7 Esther 3:13

has a defender in heaven? That explains why so many attempts to destroy them failed.

"We," say Gog and Magog, "will first join their God, and then we will destroy them."[8]

The clairvoyance of this Midrash's vision is striking. Its most perplexing facet, however, is the irrational reasoning of Gog and Magog. These nations are aware that God is persistently involved with the destiny of the Jewish People. How do they reconcile this acknowledgment with their desire to harm them? Moreover, in their pursuit to hurt, Gog and Magog plan on "joining God." Perhaps this way "He will be bribed" to support their vicious strategy. They certainly do not deny the failure of Israel's early enemies. From Esau's attempts to kill Jacob and his progeny, to Pharaoh's murderous schemes and Haman's sinister plan to exterminate the Jews, and to more of the same with medieval and contemporary leaders of various nations, God has invariably interceded to save Israel. As it were, God must wonder: "Don't these nations have any decency?" Their erratic behavior with the Chosen People defies common sense.

In reality, this unreasonable conduct is hardly surprising. It is said about Nimrod, the leader of the Tower of Babel's movement, that while he acknowledged the Master of the Universe, he consciously aimed to rebel against Him.[9] This illogical pursuit finds its source within man's essence. Man's Godly soul and earthly origin constantly pull him to either the highest achievements or to the basest animalistic instincts. The outcome of the perpetual struggle between the intellect and the physical desires generates the best or the worst in mankind. It will produce traits of nobility or foolish cruelty. The followers of evil will not desist by the knowledge of God's presence in the world and His control over large and small events.

The irrationality of this behavior should be shocking; but it is so prevalent that we are almost immune to this absurd inconsistency. Don't

---

8 Likewise, the Rambam (*Laws of Kings* 12:2) states that, at the onset of the Messianic Times, a war involving Gog and Magog will erupt.

9 Rashi, Lech Lecha

the Sages teach that even when the wicked person stands by the gate of *Gehinnom*, he obstinately refuses to repent?[10] Where physical desires rule, foolishness governs and wisdom runs away. In their blind hatred of Israel, Gog and Magog want to worship God and use Him, hoping they will succeed where other tyrants failed.

What is Am Yisrael to do during these dangerous times? Quoting the words of King David, the Midrash offers a solution.[11] "He [Hashem] will have turned to the prayer of each devastated one and not have despised their prayer. Let this be recorded for the final generation, so that the newborn people will praise God."[12] The Midrash explains that the Jews of the final generation will have neither prophets nor priests upon whom to rely, except their own prayers. Standing as a lonely tree in a dry and desolate land, the Jewish People are devastated by the silence of the surrounding nations who remain indifferent to their oppressions and condemnations. They will be under constant threats of extermination. But, during the Sukkot festival, when they take a *lulav* and *etrog* to pray, God will save them and give them a new breath of life. Moses urges Israel: "You shall take for yourselves on the first day the fruit of the citron tree, the branches of date palms, myrtle twigs, and brook willows."[13] Even if the last generation stands spiritually naked, the mitzvah of *lulav* and *etrog*, combined with prayers are enough to protect them from the wars of Gog and Magog, and to bring about their salvation. Since the war of Gog and Magog will erupt in Tishrei, the enemy will be subdued thanks to the merit of this mitzvah.[14]

On Shabbat Chol Hamoed Sukkot, we read Ezekiel's prophecy foretelling the climactic war of Gog and Magog, which introduces the End of Days and the Messianic Era. Gog, from the land of Magog, allied with a multitude of nations, will advance to attack Israel in its own land. The war will end with the destruction of Israel's enemies and the promised Messianic Era of bliss:[15] "It shall be on that day that on the day that Gog

10 BT *Eruvin* 19
11 *Midrash Rabbah*, Psalms 102:18
12 Psalms 102:18
13 Leviticus 23:40
14 *Shulchan Arukh*, 663:3, *Mishnah Brurah* 10
15 Ezekiel 38:18 39:4

comes against the soil of Israel – the word of the Lord Hashem/Elokim – My raging anger will flare up,.... You [Gog] will fall upon the mountains of Israel, you and all your cohorts and the peoples that are with you,..." By dwelling in a Sukkah for eight days, the Jews commemorate the heavenly clouds which shielded their ancestors in the Wilderness. In the Messianic Times, they will, once again, merit God's protection against the perilous menace of Gog and Magog. ■

The Etrog: An Antidote to Arrogance

When Moses sent twelve spies to explore the Land of Canaan, he selected twelve righteous individuals who also were tribe leaders.[16] Save for Joshua and Caleb, the remaining spies intentionally distorted their account and were a major disappointment. Their failure in aligning their aspirations with God's mission brought lasting tragedy upon themselves and the Jewish People. In a short time span, their status changed from greatness to infamy. What was the cause to such a dramatic spiritual degradation?[17]

Once in the Land of Canaan, the spies undertook a different mission of much higher caliber. On account of their righteousness, they sought to amend mankind's spiritual downfall brought about by Adam's original failure.[18] Through their attempted rectification, they would hasten the *tikkun olam*, for which we are still striving. How did they intend to achieve this goal?

Their first publicized act was to pick a native fruit: "They arrived at the Valley of Eshkol and cut from there a vine with one cluster of grapes, and bore it on a double pole, and of the pomegranates and of the figs."[19] What did they mean to achieve by this act? Surely, a verbal report to Moses on the exceptional fertility of the Land would be sufficient.

In reality, this act was filled with mystical significance. It was the spies' wish to rectify the earth's failure during the six days of Creation.

16 Rashi, Numbers 13:3
17 R. Friedman, *Shvilei Pinchas*, Erev Sukkot 5763
18 R. Zvi Mi'Rimanov
19 Numbers 13: 23

Then, the earth was commanded to produce fruit trees whose trunks will taste as the fruit they bore: "God said, 'Let the earth sprout vegetation: herbage yielding seed, *fruit trees yielding fruit…*'"[20] Anticipating Adam's sin, the earth disobeyed so as to become the first sinner rather than Adam, the object of Creation, thus attenuating his punishment: "And the earth brought forth vegetation: …and *trees yielding fruit,* each containing its seed after its kind." The tree trunks were unlike their fruit in looks and taste. This explains why later on the earth was also cursed along with Adam: "accursed is the ground because of you…"[21]

In disobeying God's commandment, the earth's intent was noble. It meant to provide Adam with an extenuating circumstance argument when confronted with his own failure. He could justify his weakness by pointing to the failure of the earth from where he was created: "For you are dust, and to dust shall you return."[22] During Yom Kippur, we too invoke the same argument: "Our Father, our King, remember that we are but dust." Essentially, we are building our case, saying to God: "Since the earth from where we originate disobeyed Your command, it is not surprising that we too should disappoint You."

During the spies' brief stay in the Land of Canaan, they cut a vine with one cluster of grapes. Thanks to their mystical knowledge – after all they belonged to the generation who received the Torah at Sinai – the spies wished to correct the earth's failure by causing the grapes' cluster and its branch to be equal in taste. In the process of this lofty undertaking, they got caught into the trap of *hitnas'ut,* the trait of conceitedness, and they failed (*ba-mot*). The text so testifies: "*vayisa'uhu ba-mot*" – "and bore it on a double pole," which equally translates as failure caused by haughtiness.

The latter was manifest in their drive behind the false report where they warned against conquering the Land of Israel. Contrary to their claim, their concern was not so much about the safety of their people as much as it was about upholding their leadership status. They reasoned

20 Genesis 1:11

21 Ibid., 3:17

22 Ibid., 3:19

that as long as they remain in the wilderness they will keep their title, but they will lose their perks when a new government is formed in Israel.[23]

The spies' failure is symbolized by the *etrog*'s acronym: "אל תבואני רגל גאוה"[24] – "let not the foot of arrogance come to me." According to the Midrash,[25] the *etrog* was the Tree of Knowledge to which Eve was attracted because it was the only fruit which tasted like its trunk.[26] On Sukkot, we use the etrog during our prayers as a *tikkun* for the earth's disobedience. The Torah commands: "You shall take for yourselves on the first day the fruit of the citron tree [*etrog*]."[27] In fact, Sukkot is not celebrated on the first day of the month; it is on the fifteenth day. In this context, the first day refers to the day when the earth first disobeyed God's command and produced fruit trees different from their respective trunks.

Furthermore, in a legal discussion on fulfilling the mitzvah of *etrog*, Rabbi Meir claims that it should not be smaller than the size of an almond, while Rabbi Yehudah requires a size that is not smaller than an egg and just large enough to hold two in one hand.[28] Disputing this last clause, Rabbi Yossi tells of an event when Rabbi Akiva walked into the synagogue carrying an *etrog* on his shoulder (because of its large size). Rabbi Yehudah dismissed this as proof, stating that the Sages disapproved of Rabbi Akiva's position. Why would Rabbi Akiva walk into the *shul* with a large *etrog* on his shoulder? Undoubtedly, it was to convey a lasting message.

The Talmud teaches that twenty-four thousand disciples of Rabbi Akiva died within a few weeks as a divine retribution for not acting respectfully toward each other.[29] Because of their lofty spiritual status, the *Shechinah* could not tolerate this flagrant absence of respect and unity. Subsequently, it became fitting for Rabbi Akiva, who mourned the loss of

23 Zohar, Numbers 13:3
24 Psalms 36:12
25 *Bereshit Rabbah* 15:7
26 Perhaps that in deference to God's Word, the earth produced one such tree.
27 Leviticus 23:40
28 BT *Sukkah* 34b
29 BT *Yevamot* 62b

his students more than anyone else, to teach: "You shall love your fellow Jew as yourself: this is a major tenet of the Torah, [applying even more specifically to those who learn Torah.]" When Rabbi Akiva carried a large *etrog* on his shoulder, it was to emphasize this principle. As the *etrog* symbolizes a rejection of haughtiness – "אל תבואני רגל גאוה" – "let not the foot of arrogance come to me" – Rabbi Akiva exhibited the root cause of the tragedy that befell his students and himself. The rabbis disapproved of his conduct as to say, it is no homage to their memory to display their shortcomings.

What is so horrifying about haughtiness that it should warrant a divine punishment of such a magnitude? The Sages reveal the following monologue, as it were: "About the conceited says God: He and I cannot dwell in the same world."[30] Since no being can overcome his evil inclination unless he receives God's assistance, the haughty person remains at the constant mercy of his *yetzer,* because God stays away from him. As this arrogant person is left to his own and the *yetzer's* devices, he will surely become a great sinner. So God takes him away before he becomes entrenched in sin.[31] This idea where God intervenes to take back a soul before it becomes too polluted is found with Enoch: "And Enoch walked with God; then he was no more, for God had taken him."[32]

Unlike the other three species, the *etrog*, whose fragrance and taste are pleasant, represents the Torah scholar who is crowned by his knowledge and his good character traits. On account of these great assets, the Torah scholar is more prone to feeling conceited. It is fitting that he should be warned against this danger through the symbolism enclosed within the *etrog*'s acronym: "אל תבואני רגל גאוה" – "let not the foot of arrogance come to me."

The dangers of haughtiness are unpredictably threatening. It caused the spies' demise and great harm to their generation. The *etrog* stands to remind us of these perils. ■

---

30 BT *Sotah* 5a

31 The Maharsha (*Sotah* 62b) suggests that Rabbi Akiva's students died because they did not honor the Torah of their fellow students. Since the Torah is life, "*ki hi chayecha,*" then they were deprived of life, as a measure for measure.

32 Rashi, Genesis 5:24

Happiness Is Independent of Mundane Pursuits

Referring to the Midrash's declaration that every plant which grows on our planet is under the supervision of its specific angel,[33] the Chidah suggests that the *arba minim* do not fall under this rule.[34] Their growth is directly under God's *hashgacha*, and as such, they represent God's scepter which we, His children, are granted permission to handle. Although a king may not forgo the proper protocol due to him, and thus no one can use his scepter, a father on the other hand, may forgo his honor. During Rosh Hashana and Yom Kippur, our relationship with God is on a king to servant level, but on Sukkot, a new development takes place – the liaison is between a father and son.[35] Since He is "*avinu*," we carry His scepter – the four species – to show the mutual love that prevails between us and God.

Therefore, we are commanded to "rejoice before Hashem" during the celebration of Sukkot.[36] The root cause for the rejoicing is God's love toward Am Yisrael. One can grasp this true moment of happiness only when he consecrates his intellectual faculties to God while giving little or no attention to the worldly pleasures. This also explains why we leave the comfort of our homes to dwell in the Sukkah. It is to walk away from the mundane luxuries and meditate on our unique relationship with God. Through these solemn moments of solitude, we will experience the happiness of Sukkot.

Individually, the four species symbolize the body parts most susceptible to the physical pleasures of life. The willow branches (*aravot*) resemble the lips, the myrtle leaves (*hadassim*) look like the eye, the citron (*etrog*) is compared to the heart, and the palm branch (*lulav*) represents the spinal cord which links the brain to the lower bodily parts. In life, man's material desires are initiated by the sight, the mouth, the heart and the brain. As Sukkot is a "festival of Hashem,"[37] we are urged to dedicate

---

33 *Bereshit Rabbah* 10:7.

34 *Rosh David*, Emor 347.

35 R. Berzovsky, *Netivot Shalom*, *Makor Hasimcha*

36 Leviticus 23:40

37 Ibid., 23:41

our physical senses – represented by the four species – to reach spiritual heights in order to find true happiness.

It is thanks to the exalted joy experienced during Sukkot that many reached the level of prophecy in the days of Beit Hamikdash, since the state of prophecy settles only in a joyful heart. We find that King Saul insisted that David plays the harp in the palace, hoping to experience prophecy through happiness. The nightly festive celebrations of *Simchat Beit Hasho'evah* gained legendary status in the heightened feeling of joy. Through this feeling, many drew (*sho'evah*) upon themselves the supernatural sensation of prophecy.

As to highlight the significance of achieving happiness, the Sages tell a story about a king who fell gravely ill. As all his physicians despaired, a wise man hinted at a hopeful way out. The king can only be cured if he wears the cloak of the happiest man in the kingdom. After a lengthy national search, the king's advisors' finally found a man in constant state of happiness without the slightest worry. As they explained to him the urgency of the situation, he calmly replied that he does not own a cloak and that his happiness would be hindered if he had owned anything of value.

The Mussar teachers wanted to relay that unless one detaches himself from the materialistic pursuits of this world, he or she cannot achieve real happiness. The latter is impeded by common human attitudes such as jealousy, lust and search for prestige. While certain mundane pursuits are essential in life, they must not supplant the true objective of life's mission, namely, to worship God *b'simcha*, with joy. ■

Sukkot Is a Time for Teshuvah Out of Love

The Arizal explains that during Sukkot, God reveals Himself to *Klal Yisrael* through His Name "*El*," defining kindness. What does that mean?[38]

According to Jewish Law, one who is legally bound to provide food for someone else does not have to offer clothing, but when a person is

38 R. Friedman, *Shvilei Pinchas*, Sukkot 5769

mandated to supply clothing, he implicitly must offer food also.[39] As we celebrate Sukkot to commemorate the heavenly clouds which shielded the Israelites in the Wilderness, and since these clouds washed clean the Israelites' clothing during the forty-year-long journey,[40] it follows that God is equally committed to grant Am Yisrael all its food requirements.[41] This *kal vachomer*, where a more stringent rule is deducted from a lenient situation, and vice versa, is one of the thirteen principles through which legal deductions are derived in the Torah.[42] They correspond to the thirteen attributes of divine compassion which we repeatedly recite on Yom Kippur.[43] *El*, the first attribute (according to the Arizal) which invokes divine kindness, corresponds to *kal vachomer*, the first of the thirteen principles of legal deductions.

Similarly, when Moses prayed on behalf of Miriam, he too called on the divine name *El*: "*El nah refah nah lah*" – "Please, Hashem, heal her now."[44] God had hinted to Moses the propitious timing for invoking the divine name *El* by raising a *kal vachomer*: "Were her father to spit in her face, would she not be humiliated for seven days? [How much more so when I am angry at her that] she should be quarantined outside the camp for seven days…" Consequently, during Sukkot, when sustenance flows through *kal vachomer*, the first of the thirteen principles of legal deductions, God interacts with Am Yisrael with kindness through the divine name *El*,[45] the first of the thirteen attributes of divine mercy.

It is noteworthy to point at the apparent discrepancy found in the last of the thirteen attributes of divine compassion: "ונקה לא ינקה" – "and Who Cleanses – but does not cleanse completely."[46]

---

39 *Choshen Mishpat* 60:3
40 Deuteronomy 8:4: "Your garment did not wear out upon you…, these forty years"
41 *Midrash Shocher Tov*, Psalms 23
42 *Torat Kohanim* 1
43 The Magid MiMezritch
44 Numbers 12:13
45 The Arizal, *Shaar Chag Hasukkot* 1
46 Exodus 34:7

Says the Talmud: "God wipes out the sins of the repentant, but not the sins of those who do not repent."[47] Really, this last restriction has no place with the attributes of compassion, according to which all sins must be forgiven without qualifications. The Arizal reconciles this contradiction through a twist with the Mishna's words: "אל תסתכל בקנקן אלא במה שיש בו" – "Do not look at the vessel, but what is in it," a cautious note to avoid passing judgment based on outside appearance.[48] In the case of "ונקה לא ינקה" found in the thirteen attributes, if we extract the letters נק and נק we end up with the word "קנקן" – vessel. The remaining letters form the Divine Name *yud key vav key*. So, one should not focus on the literal meaning of "ונקה לא ינקה" "and Who Cleanses – but does not cleanse completely." Rather look at what is in it, the Divine Name of compassion *yud key vav key*. God acts with kindness toward those who repent out of fear of retribution, a lower form of *teshuvah*, in the same way He favors those who repent out of love for Him. To the latter, He transforms their sins into merits – ונקה – and He cleanses. To the former, He waits for a higher form of *teshuvah* – לא ינקה – but does not cleanse completely – until they return to God with love, at which time He will count their transgressions as *mitzvot*.

Now, we can address the question of the Midrash on the command to acquire on the first day of Sukkot the four species:[49] "You shall take for yourselves on the first day, the fruit of a citron tree, the branches of date palms."[50] Why does the Torah refer to it as the first day? Sukkot begins on the fifteenth of the month. Answers the Midrash: It is the first day for the counting of the sins [following Yom Kippur]. As God reveals Himself to Am Yisrael through *El*, His name of Kindness, the first day of Sukkot is when He transforms our transgressions into merits. On Rosh Hashana and Yom Kippur, our *teshuvah* was marked by personal motives, the fear of retribution,[51] so God holds onto our sins until the first day of Sukkot, a day of rejoicing, when our *teshuvah* is marked by our love for God. Then, all our sins are turned into *zechuyot*, merits.

---

47 BT *Yomah* 86a

48 *Avot* 4:27 "Do not look at the vessel, but what is in it; there is a new vessel filled with old wine and an old vessel that does not even contain new wine." (One should not judge others by their appearance only.)

49 *Tanchumah*, Emor 22

50 Leviticus 23:40

51 *Kedushat Halevy*, Vayelech

In reality, this astonishing concept of turning the sinner's actions into good deeds sounds illogical at best if not bizarre, until we consider the following Gemara: "Rabbi Hama son of Rabbi Hanina taught that were it not for the following three verses, Am Yisrael would definitely be pronounced guilty in heaven with no redeeming chances: "On that day – the word of Hashem – I will assemble the lame one and gather in the one driven away and whomever I have harmed" (Micah 4:6).[52] How has God harmed Am Yisrael? It is because He created the *yetzer hara* who has misled the Jewish People. As it were, God feels some responsibility for Israel's failure. Somehow, He was a major contributor by creating the Evil forces. However, when a Jew does *teshuvah* for God's sake and not out of fear, he acknowledges that God's Creation is perfect – to include the *yetzer hara* whose goal is to help man exercise his free will for his ultimate benefit. As it were, man's *teshuvah* is a vindication of God's Creation of the *yetzer*. This in turn gives *nachat* to God. So for this individual God reverses all the sins to merits, to show that in the end the creation of the *yetzer hara* has indeed benefited man. ■

Sukkot Counters Evil

The main role of the Evil Inclination has always been to harm Israel. Being the People of the Book, who carry on Earth the divine message and the flame of spirituality and holiness, Evil's goal along with that of the many nations who unjustly torment the Jewish People consist in extinguishing that torch of truth.[53] This destructive spirit is driven by Satan and his female counterpart, mystically known as לילית – Lilith. The latter spreads its devastation through 480 legions that are under its control. The numerical value of the Hebrew word *Lilit* equals 480.

However, on Yom Kippur שטן – Satan, whose numerical value is 364, is powerless against Am Yisrael. For three hundred and sixty four days of

52 BT Brachot 32a. The next two verses equally demonstrate that God holds the ability to subdue our *yetzer*. "Can I not do to you, O House of Israel, what this potter does? – the word of Hashem. Behold, just as clay is in the hand of the potter, so are you in My hand, O House of Israel" (Jeremiah 18:6). "I will give you a new heart and put a new spirit within you; I will remove the heart of stone from your flesh and give you a heart of flesh" (Ezekiel 36:26).

53 R. Zvi Hirsh Kaidanver, *Kav HaYashar*, chap. 95

the year, Satan prosecutes Am Yisrael, except on the Day of Atonement. On this day, the Jewish heart is unaffected by the worldly temptations and turns with full dedication to the Creator.

What this means is that at the conclusion of Yom Kippur, the *yetzer* will immediately resume its harmful influence. So in order to avoid falling into the traps laid by the *yetzer*, we are commanded to start building the Sukkah that same night.[54] It is because the numerical value for the Hebrew word Sukkot, (סכת) equals 480. The holiness of this commandment will keep in check the 480 camps which operate under the damaging rule of Lilith.

Likewise, during the times of the Beit Hamikdash, there were 480 houses of worship in Jerusalem, which, when we include the Temple, add to 481. Their holiness countered the damages wrecked by Lilith which represented the 480 camps of destruction. It is so alluded in the Prophet's words: "How the faithful city [Jerusalem] have become a harlot! – She had been full of justice, (מלאתי משפט) righteousness lodged in her, but now murderers!"[55] Again, the numerical value of מלאתי adds to 481. As long as righteousness was present in Jerusalem, it was filled with justice. But when Jerusalem was destroyed, Lilith's destructive power overwhelmingly grew to cause a killing spree in the streets of the holy city. The murderous sword of the Babylonian invaders became Lilith instrument.

Considering all these facts, one must not lightly treat the mitzvah of Sukkot as it represents an antidote to Evil. Thus in Messianic Times, when the nations will argue that God neglected them by not giving them the Torah, He will suggest as a test to their motivation that they observe the holiday of Sukkot. Then God will bring forth an extremely hot sun, and the Gentiles will impatiently kick their Sukkah and walk away. We see that of all the beautiful Torah commandments, God will challenge the nations, only with the mitzvah of Sukkah. As this commandment counterbalances Evil, it is indeed very dear in God's Eyes.

It is so because, in Messianic Times, all the false ideologies will be exposed and destroyed so that God's Oneness will be acknowledged by

---

54 *Shulchan Arukh* 624:5

55 Isaiah 1:21

all mankind. Lilith and its forces will be completely subdued thanks to fulfilling the Sukkah commandment. Then, Jerusalem will be once more, מלאתי משפט – a city full of justice, as the Beit Hamikdash along with the 480 houses of worship shall return to their previous glory. ■

THE FOUR SPECIES SYMBOLIZE THE AVOIDANCE OF SIN

The observance of the *arba minim*, four species, which must be acquired for the first day of Sukkot, is mentioned in the following verse: "You shall take for yourselves on the first day, the fruit of the citron tree, the branches of date palms, myrtle twigs, and brook willows; and you shall rejoice before Hashem, your God, for a seven-day period."[56] Elaborating on the qualification of the fifteenth day of the month of Tishrei as the first day, our Sages explain that it is the first day of the year when our sins start to accumulate. Yom Kippur has just passed, and we hopefully emerged with a clean slate, while we try to carry its spiritual benefits. With the *arba minim*, the Torah offers a remedy to potential failures.[57]

The fruit of a citron tree is a euphemism for *shemirat ha-brit*, the sanctification of the *brit*, which refer to laws pertaining to prohibited relations. If these laws are not observed, all of one's *mitzvot* and good deeds are to no avail. Worse, they feed and strengthen the forces of evil. The core element of *avodat Hashem* consists of guarded conjugal behavior in line with the Torah commandments. The numerical value of *etrog* in Hebrew is equal to that of the word *brit*, which is 612. The *brit* is represented by the *etrog*, also called "*pri eitz hadar*" – "the fruit of a beautiful tree." Man, who is also compared to a tree, must preserve his spiritual beauty through the sanctity of the *brit*.

The branches of the date palms – or the *lulav*, symbolize the heart. The heart is preoccupied with numerous disturbing thoughts just as the palm tree is filled with abundant dates. Now that a new tally is about to start, we have to purify our hearts and dedicate our thoughts to God and emulate the righteous, who are compared to the date.

---

56 Leviticus 23:40

57 R. Abuchatzeira, *Pituchei Chotam*, Emor

The myrtle twigs, the *hadas*, are eye-shaped. It invokes the duties of the eyes. A person should protect his eyes from seeing impure and forbidden sights that would tempt him or lead him to commit sinful acts. Just as the tree leaf shields the fruit, so too must our eyelids restrict the eyes to look only at what is permitted. The essence of man is defined by his thoughts, and they result from his sightings.

Arvei nachal, brook willows, resemble the shape of our lips. When a person gives free rein to his speech and talks without restraint, his words become meaningless in the same way these brook willows are without fragrance. Not only must one not speak evil, but he must also avoid senseless talk. Furthermore, the numerical value of *arvei nachal* in Hebrew is equal to that of *zeh nachash* – 370. One who doesn't guard his speech draws upon himself the influence of the *nachash* (serpent), which personifies the forces of evil, and then he is more likely to sin. In contrast, one who controls his speech will deserve to be guided by the *Shechinah,* the Divine Presence.

It is said that once a Roman ruler sent, as a sign of friendship, a precious stone to Rabbeinu Hakadosh. To reciprocate the friendship gesture, the rabbi sent back a *mezuzah*. The Roman governor was not pleased as he compared the priceless value of the gem to the parchment in his hands. Rabbeinu Hakadosh explained that it would provide protection to his family. At that time, the governor's only daughter was seriously ill and the doctors gave up on saving her life. Then the governor put the *mezuzah* next to his daughter and she recovered. Likewise, the four species look like simple plants, but they carry valuable messages to help us refine our character traits. By guarding our speech, thoughts and sightings, and by restraining our physical desires, we will undoubtedly succeed in being the *eved Hashem*, God's servant, that He wants us to become. ■

COUNTERACTING THE EVIL OF THE FOUR KINGDOMS

Rabbeinu Bechai explains that the four species – *lulav*, *etrog*, *hadas* and *aravah* – correspond to the kingdoms of Babylon, Persia, Greece and Rome.[58] Throughout history, Israel was exiled and subjugated by these

58 *Shem MiShmuel*, *Sukkot* 179

four nations. At the same time, the Maharal suggests that these four kingdoms symbolize the evil forces which drive idol worship, illicit relations, spilling of blood and *lashon hara* (evil speech). The latter, being as consequential in severity as the first three put together. This explains the seemingly unending exile under Rome represented by Christianity. Israel's tribulations during the past two thousand years reflect the gravity of *lashon hara* which drives a deep wedge into the unity of the Jewish People. When a Jew speaks evil about his neighbor, he invites prosecuting angels in heaven to equally prosecute him. As it were, during that moment, God is forced to listen to their arguments. The potential harm which these four nations are capable to inflict is far beyond what has been witnessed to date. It is the merits of the four species which keep in check the evil promoted by these nations. That is why Israel is given this commandment: "You shall take for yourselves on the first day the fruit of the citron tree, the branches of date palms, myrtle twigs, and brook willows; and you shall rejoice before Hashem, your God, for a seven-day period."[59]

The Zohar adds that God's Name *alef dalet nun yud* which proclaims God's Kingship, corresponds to Rosh Hashana's message, namely to weaken the forces promoting idol worship and to atone for this sin. Yom Kippur corresponds to the Divine Name *yud key vav key*. It atones for the sin of prohibited relations. Sukkot causes atonement for the spilling of blood. The holiness of these three holidays stands as an antithesis to the forces of evil embodied by Babylon, Persia and Greece. As to the harmful influence of Rome, it will be countered by Israel's unity. Considering that the last exile was brought about by senseless hatred, it can be rectified by unrestrained kindness. So, by observing these holidays, Israel reduces the impact of these four cardinal sins and spreads into the world goodness and Godliness.

Likewise, through the merit of *lulav* and *etrog*, the forces of idol worship and illicit relations are weakened, in the same manner that they are countered by the sanctity of Rosh Hashana and Yom Kippur. The *hadas* is composed of grouped leaves, representing the unity between the body and soul; it stands to counter the spilling of blood which interrupts that unity. The *aravot* are shaped like the lips and fight the forces of evil gossip.

59 Leviticus 23:40

Moreover, the merits of these three holidays and the four species give a Jew a spiritual boost to reach a high level of *teshuvah*. In exile, while we lack the guidance of our priests and Levites, and we remain exposed to the ideologies of the four nations, the powerful sanctity of the holidays and four species form a spiritual shield against their influence. ■

Shemini Atzeret

SHEMINI ATZERET

Unlike Passover, Shavuot or Sukkot, no reason is given in the Torah as to why we celebrate Shemini Atzeret on the eighth day. Its kedusha *is above the laws of nature. It is likened to the parchment upon which the Torah letters are inscribed. Its holiness is superior to the Torah letters themselves. Now we can appreciate the Zohar's statement about this holiday: it is the* gmar chatima, *the conclusion of our judgment which began on Rosh Hashana. As we joyfully dance with the Torah on Shemini Atzeret, we earn the merit of being inscribed in the Book of Life, thanks to a surge of love toward God.*

GRATITUDE OF ACCEPTING THE TORAH

Throughout the world, Jewish communities joyfully dance with Torah scrolls on Shemini Atzeret. Copious meals are served in a spirit of rejoicing and unity, and mostly with a feeling of abundant gratitude to God for giving us His precious Torah. This is the day of Simchat Torah which falls on the 22nd of Tishrei, although it is equally celebrated on the 23rd of Tishrei outside Eretz Yisrael. In reality, this celebration should take place five months earlier, in Sivan, as it is the time when the Torah was first given at Sinai. So, why do we hold this event five months later?[1]

A story is told of a princess who, when she came of age to marry, asked her father to find her a commoner with good character traits. She did not want to marry into royalty or aristocracy. Rather, she explained, she wants to live with someone who is humble and truthful. She could not bear to spend her life with a vain and haughty man, she added. Impressed by the subtle wisdom of the princess, the king acquiesced to his daughter's wish and delegated the delicate task to his most trusted advisors. They soon embarked on a journey to canvass the kingdom in search of a fitting bridegroom.

During a brief stay in a small village, the noblemen's attention was drawn to a young and attractive shepherd. Following a few meetings and private conversations, the advisors were impressed by the young man and unanimously concluded that he will be the perfect husband for the princess. They convinced the young man to follow them to the palace where he was introduced to the king. Within a few days, the shepherd made as good an impression on the king as on the advisors. The young man's qualities and refined character traits were indeed exemplary.

The king lost no time and proposed his daughter for marriage to the shepherd. The latter was literally stupefied. Nonetheless, he had to abide by the king's unexpected proposal. Within a short time, he was married and lived happily with his new bride.

1 R. Aharon Zakai, *Drashot LaMoadim*

However, a year later, this fortunate villager approached the king and indicated that he would like to marry his daughter. "You are already married to my daughter!" exclaimed the perplexed King.

"Your Majesty," said the son-in-law, "a year ago, I suspected that your daughter had some major mental problems and character deficiencies, and that was the reason I was coerced into marrying her; however, now I realize that my suspicions were unfounded and that she is as beautiful inside as she is from outside. So today, it is my sincere desire to marry her and to spend my life with her." Hearing these sweet words, the king was pleased and arranged for another happy celebration.

When, at Sinai, the Children of Israel received the Torah, they too were stupefied. Although they accepted the Torah, they did not know as yet, its inherent beauty. It took a few months before they began to appreciate the infinite splendor of the Torah. Then, Shemini Atzeret was designated as the day of Simchat Torah, a genuine rejoicing.

The initial hesitation of Am Yisrael at Sinai is understandable. The spiritual exaltedness of the Torah dictates that it should be given to the angelic world, rather than to man who is prone to sin because of his Evil Inclination.[2] In fact, the Talmud relates the fascinating debate which took place between God, the angels, and Moses when he went up to receive the Torah:[3]

"Master of the Universe" exclaimed the ministering angels! "How could You give to a human being this precious treasure – the Torah – which was carefully guarded in Your coffers for 974 generations prior to Creation? Let Your glory remain in Heaven!"

God asked Moses to respond! Moses indicated that he feared the angels' fiery breath.

"Hold onto My Glorious Throne and respond to their argument!" said God.

2 R. Friedman, *Shvilei Pinchas*, Erev Rosh Hashana 5768

3 BT *Shabbat* 88b

Then, Moses proceeded to weaken the angels' reasoning. "Master of the Universe! What is written in the Torah? You shall not kill, you shall not commit adultery, you shall not steal [prohibition against kidnapping]. Do the feelings of jealousy and competition apply to angels? Is the Evil Inclination part of their world?" Then, the ministering angels withdrew their early opposition and agreed to God's decision.

At first, it seemed that the ministering angels had a valid argument. The Torah should really stay in a place free from Evil. Yet, Moses won his case by attacking precisely the angel's claim. The ultimate objective of Creation consists in proclaiming God's Kingship over mankind. The Seraphim and Ofanim are not able to achieve this goal because there is no Evil within their ranks. Without struggle, they accept the yoke of heaven. Only Am Yisrael will employ its faculty of choice to battle a powerful evil force, and to acknowledge God as its King.[4] This is the reason God gave the Torah to the Jewish People. He knew that – through them and notwithstanding the seemingly insurmountable challenges such as the temptations of Evil, the persecutions, and the exiles – His Name shall be revealed to the entire world.

King David urges people to check out the Torah: "Contemplate and see that Hashem is good."[5] Someone who was raised outside the world of Torah will never appreciate its goodness unless he comes forward to "taste" it. It is also King David who, despite all the material riches he possessed, declared: "One thing I asked of Hashem, that shall I seek: Would that I dwell in the house of Hashem all the days of my life..."[6] This was King David's best wish: to spend all his life within the walls of a Beit Midrash and learn Torah. Many dedicate twelve to sixteen years of their life studying various secular disciplines, albeit important subjects but stay shy from God's message to mankind. Had they been aware of the piercing beauty and logic of the Torah they would make Torah study their life's priority, as indeed God wishes us to.

A story is told about a rabbi and a secular Jew who travelled by train from Haifa to Tel-Aviv. Throughout the journey, the secular Jew pestered

---

4 The *yetzer hara* unleashes its daily attacks mostly against the Jewish People on account of the holiness of their Torah.

5 Psalms 34:9

6 Ibid., 27:4

the rabbi with mocking remarks about the need to observe dietary laws, Shabbat rites, family purity regulations and so on at the onset of the 21st century. According to his logic, the time has come to drop all these constraints and to live along with the modern developments of the society at large. Why do you need this and what benefit do we gain from such a law, he argued with a cynical grin?

Finally, when the train approached its destination, the rabbi asked his companion about his occupation. The latter was proud to display architectural drawings of a major project in downtown Tel-Aviv. It was for a high rise twin towers which he designed. Then, the rabbi proceeded to suggest some changes. The architect was furious.

"How dare you make suggestions about a complicated topic of which you know nothing!" he outrageously stated. "For the past thirty years, I have been the top architect of the country!" he added with indignation.

The rabbi calmly responded: "After thirty years you are not willing to tolerate any interference with your expertise, so how do you take the liberty to interfere with our Torah which is 3,300 years old?" Then, when the Torah was given to Israel, God had foreseen corporate office culture, fast lane freeways and electronic cells which will activate escalators. Still, Torah observance was never made conditional upon man's inventions and scientific progress.

Across the world, whenever a Jew is called to the Torah on Shabbat, he recites the following blessing: "Blessed are You, Hashem, our God, King of the universe, Who chose us from among all the nations and gave us His Torah. Blessed are You, Hashem, Who gives the Torah." Indeed, Simchat Torah is the culmination of our heartfelt gratitude to God for giving us the Torah for which the angels unsuccessfully vied. ■

THE UNIQUENESS OF SHEMINI ATZERET

Shemini Atzeret is simply known as the eighth day with no historical justification. On Passover, we celebrate the Exodus from Egypt, while on Shavuot we recall the Giving of the Torah at Sinai, and during Sukkot we commemorate the heavenly clouds which as a protective shield from the heat and chills of the Wilderness hovered over the Jewish People for forty years. So, what is the true significance of Shemini Atzeret?[7]

There are three ideas associated with Shemini Atzeret. An additional dimension of closeness to God is the most prevalent concept. Following Rosh Hashana, Yom Kippur and Sukkot, God expresses a wish, as it were, to spend one more day with Am Yisrael.[8] It is a manifestation of mutual love between God and His people. Also, according to the Zohar, this day represents the *gmar hatima*,[9] finalizing our judgment which began on Rosh Hashana. Finally, it is a day when the reading of the Torah cycle is completed which drives a well-established custom for joyous celebrations.[10]

The Maharal adds that the status of this holiday is above the laws of nature which are all constrained within the well-known cycle of seven.[11] On the eighth day, one reaches higher spiritual levels from which all material pursuits are inconsequential. As an illustration, it is on the eighth day that the circumcision commandment is observed. It is only when an individual rises above the laws of nature that he or she will readily abide by all ordinances prescribed by the Supreme Being.

So, while Passover and Sukkot are each limited to a seven day commemoration, Shemini Atzeret takes place on the eighth day, calling for a greater spiritual mindset which will lead us to void our physical essence and aspire to cling to God. Thus all other holidays lead to Shemini Atzeret as an eye-opener to a world above nature, the World to Come.

Likewise, there are three celebrations which are associated with the concept represented by the eighth day. Shavuot occurs at the conclusion of the counting of seven weeks of the Omer. It is a time of introspection to purify ourselves before accepting anew the Torah. Similarly, the High Priest readies himself for seven days prior to Yom Kippur when he enters

---

7 R. Berzovsky, *Netivot Shalom*, Simchat Torah 1

8 BT *Sukkah* 55b

9 Zohar I, 220a

10 Zohar III, 256b

11 Maharal, *Drasha L'Shabbat Tshuvah*

the Holy of Holies in Beit Hamikdash. On these occasions, our closeness to God is achieved through meditation, intense prayers and fasting. However, on Shemini Atzeret, our closeness to God is realized through dancing and singing. These three celebrations, which do not require any physical act, are a strong proof of our love of God. They are the *hotam al libecha*, the seal of love that Am Yisrael carries within its heart for God. Unlike Sukkot, which requires building a temporary dwelling along with acquiring the *lulav* and *etrog*, and unlike Pesach which involves the matzah consumption, and unlike Rosh Hashana when the *shofar* is blown, Shemini Atzeret simply stirs our sentiment of gratitude and love toward God. In our relation with God, Sukkot evokes the idea of "Many waters of heathen tribulations cannot extinguish the fire of this love."[12] Yet Shemini Atzeret reveals a higher dimension in this eternal relationship: "for strong till the death is my love."[13] It is this admirable attribute that makes Shemini Atzeret, where "*atzeret*" translates into gathering, an all inclusive celebration representing the symbolisms of all the other holidays.

Thus unlike Passover, Shavuot or Sukkot, no reason is given in the Torah as to why we celebrate this holiday. Shemini Atzeret's *kedusha* is above the laws of nature. It is likened to the parchment upon which the Torah letters are inscribed.[14] Its holiness is superior to the Torah letters themselves.

Now we can appreciate the Zohar's statement about this holiday: it is the *gmar hatima*, the conclusion of our judgment which began on Rosh Hashana. On Shemini Atzeret, one earns the merit of being inscribed in the Book of Life thanks to a surge of love toward God. ■

12 Song of Songs 8:7

13 Ibid., 8:6

14 *Noam Elimelech*

Chanukah

CHANUKAH

Inside the Temple were two vessels of the highest significance. The Ark contained the Testimonial-tablets representing the Written Torah, and the Menorah of pure gold whose lights symbolized the Oral Torah. Under the leadership of Moses, the first Sanctuary was built in the Wilderness because God wanted to dwell in the midst of Am Yisrael in the same way His presence descended upon Mount Sinai.[1] *So for forty years, both aspects of the Torah – the written and the oral – flourished through two faithful emissaries: Moses and Aaron, the High Priest. For forty years, Aaron was in charge of lighting the Menorah every day, symbolizing man's personal efforts and intellectual pursuits to understanding and upholding the Oral Law. It is through the Menorah lights, representing the Oral Torah, that God grants the Sages the authority to issue additional ordinances or decrees. Is God not the light to the entire universe? Why does He ask the High Priest to light a few more flames? It is God's desire to dwell in the midst of Israel, and because He eagerly awaits the deeds of the righteous – symbolized by the lights of Chanukah – to trigger the flow of divine blessings upon the world.*

1 Ramban, Terumah

ANCIENT GREECE REJECTED THE LIGHT OF SPIRITUALITY

"When the earth was astonishingly empty, with darkness upon the surface of the deep, and the Divine Spirit hovered upon the surface of the waters."[2] In addition to portraying the pre-creation scenery, this verse, says the Midrash, also foretells the tumultuous history of the Jewish People.[3] "When the earth was astonishingly empty" refers to the Jewish exile under both the Babylonian kingdom and the Persian Empire. "With darkness upon the surface" describes the Jewish oppression under the yoke of the Greek Empire. "The surface of the deep" refers to the fourth exile under Edom which, like the ocean's depth, continues unabated with no end in sight. "And the Divine Spirit hovered upon the surface of the waters" – that is the spirit of Mashiach who is awaiting our repentance which is likened to water.

The wickedness of these four kingdoms describes the evil that will plague Creation from its dawn until the Messianic days.[4] The ills of the world whose natures are identified with the unique characteristics of each one of these four nations will travel across space and time to bring misery and unhappiness to mankind.

Moreover, the characteristics of these four kingdoms correspond to four sins: the three cardinal sins over which one must be willing to die rather than commit, and to slanderous speech. Babylon is identified with idol worship, while Persia is defined by its immoral conjugal acts. Greece, the nation who sought to enlighten the world is linked by the Torah Sages to the sin of killing. How do we explain this analogy? It stands in contradiction with that culture's glorification of the body and intellect! Spilling blood means taking the life from a body which is now deprived of its animation.[5] Greece promoted the cult of personality and physical strength. It translated the Torah to show its external beauty, but it showed disdain for the *pnimiyut*, the religious depth of the Torah. This is likened to blood spilling which causes loss of life. Without the *pnimiyut* of the Torah, the spiritual life is gone and the connection with God is ruptured.

---

2 Genesis 1:2

3 *Bereshit Rabbah* 82:5

4 R. Sherer *Ohr Gedaliahu*, Jerusalem: 1990, Chanukah 1

5 Maharal, *Netzach Yisrael*

That is why the Sages have harsher words for one who misleads his fellow to sin, than for one who kills him. The former, where spiritual life is cut short, is treated as murder for eternity. This is a worse form of the spilling of blood. Therefore, Greece's philosophy is labeled *hochmah hitzonit*, an external wisdom deprived of inner spirituality. It is this failed way of life they forced upon the Jews. Finally, Rome's flagrant arrogance corresponds to the irrational hatred which pervaded Jewish societies during the times of the Second Temple. Senseless slander originates from haughtiness and can only be repaired by unreserved kindness and love.

The three Patriarchs instilled their primary attributes into their descendants to spiritually sustain them for future generations. Abraham's attribute of loving-kindness promoted holiness, and counterbalanced the destructive effects of immorality. Isaac weakened idol worship through the unparalleled fear with which he served the awesome God. Jacob's attribute is *emet*, truth, which defies the spilling of blood. Falsehood is defined by a discrepancy between inner thoughts and outer conduct. On the other hand, truth reflects a perfect harmony between inner spiritual strength and external behavior. It is said about Jacob that never in his life did he experience an unwarranted seminal emission, thus he demonstrated in the highest manner the value of life, in opposition to the spilling of blood and falsehood upheld by the Greeks. It is in the merit of Yaakov Avinu that the Hasmoneans were able to overcome the Greek's menace.

The Hellenist period is known as darkness because the Greek rulers issued cruel decrees threatening the soul of the Jewish People. Although the Israelites lived in their land under the enlightenment of their Sages, the enemy sought to suppress that guidance. The Greeks had no quarrel with the Temple or with the Torah. On the contrary, they translated the Torah into seventy languages, made it available to everyone and publicized its splendor. But they wanted Israel to live on its land and behave like all other nations. The Hellenists dismissed the *pnimiyut*, spiritual depth of the Torah and the Temple. They rejected the Sages' tradition and ordered the Jews to inscribe upon the ox's horn "that we have no part in the God of Israel." Through this inscription, the invaders reminded Israel of their early wish to worship the golden calf.[6]

6 Ramban, Ki Tissa

The Greeks' destructive intent was made clear through the translation of the Torah into other languages. They wished to void the concept of *hashgacha pratit*, constant divine control over nature and the course of life. Through the translation, they proclaimed that the Jewish nation is like all other nations. This is why – as a heavenly sign of displeasure – darkness enveloped the world for three days following the translation of the Torah.

The unique and historical relationship between Israel and God was anathema to the Greeks. Their ideology categorically opposed that association best described with these words: "They saw the God of Israel, and under His feet was the likeness of sapphire brickwork, and it was like the essence of heaven in purity."[7] This verse underlines the special relationship which always exists between God and the Jewish People. As it were, bricks are in God's vicinity, reminding Him of the Jews' suffering, while the appearance of heaven's purity recalls the joy of their eventual deliverance.[8] The Jewish People are aware that even at the peak of their sufferings, they are under God's *hashgacha*. Greatness results from exile, a state of purification. Eventually, the bricks will shine like a sapphire. The Hellenists rejected this idea and forced the Jews to inscribe on the ox's horn "that we have no part in the God of Israel."

During their rule, the Hellenists issued three decrees to weaken the Jewish religion. They forbade the Jews to circumcise, to proclaim the New Moon and to observe Shabbat. Through the first decree, they sought to eliminate the physical distinction that existed between a Jew and a Greek. The holiness of the *brit* points to the holiness of the body and to a controlled enjoyment of the material life. The Greeks' culture essentially highlighted the unobstructed access to the body's desires. Also, the proclamation of the New Moon indicates the sanctity of time, but most importantly, that God has set Israel in control of time. Through this remarkable concept, Israel, not God, decides when Yom Kippur or Passover will fall. "Hashem said to Moses and Aaron in the land of Egypt, saying, 'This month shall be for you…'"[9] As it were, God delegated to Israel the control over time

7 Exodus 24:10
8 BT *Sotah* 12
9 Exodus 12:1

and nature's course.[10] This too set Israel above the laws of nature and of any other nation. Again, the Greeks were set to uproot this unnatural idea. As to Shabbat, it revealed a fascinating dimension within Creation – that of *Olam Habbah*, which the Greeks negated at all costs.

The challenges the Hasmoneans confronted were not unique to their generation. The darkness of alien cultures still surrounds us, and is commonly encountered with the modern day Hellenists who err in their claim: "My strength and the might of my hand made me all this wealth!"[11] The lights of the Menorah along with the heroic spirit of the Hasmoneans remind us that we can, with certainty, overcome darkness. Most importantly, they remind us that it is not the strong which runs the world, rather it is the God of Israel. ■

Conveying God's Love with a Flask of Oil

What is Chanukah? The Talmud answers this question by focusing on the miracle of the oil flask.[12] When the Hellenists took over the Holy Temple in Jerusalem, they defiled the oils used to light the Menorah. When the Hasmoneans regained control over the Temple, they found a small flask of oil sealed by the High Priest signet which had not been defiled. In a miraculous way, the quantity of oil that should have lit for just one day, lit for eight days. The following year, the Sages instituted eight days of celebration and praise to God over the oil's miracle.

As we see, the main reason for observing Chanukah hovers around the small quantity of oil which unexpectedly lit for a longer period.[13] Yet, during those years of darkness, the Jewish People faced dangerous prospects of annihilation by the cruel invaders. The Hellenists methodically devised ways of eliminating Judaism altogether. It is thanks to the heroic self-sacrifice of the Hasmoneans – a small, untrained group of priests – that the Jewish People was miraculously saved. In His great compassion, God delivered the many into the hands of the few, the strong into the hands of

10 Sforno, Ibid.
11 Deuteronomy 8:17
12 BT*Shabbat* 21a
13 R. Chaim Shmuelevitz, *Sichot Mussar*, 16,

the weak, the wicked into the hands of the righteous. The miracle of the oil pales in comparison to the true miracle that saved an entire nation from a powerful, well-trained and well-equipped army. It is thanks to the divine intervention on behalf of a weak band of priests that Am Yisrael was saved. Reason necessitates that the Talmud Sages would call for a celebration on this account alone rather than on account of the oil flask.

Undoubtedly, the true miracle over which we ought to praise God is the salvation He granted the Jewish People. When so many nations crumbled under the sword of the evil Greek Empire, God took up the Jews' fight and the enemy was defeated. While the miracle of the oil was unnecessary, God proceeded with it anyway, as a show of love to Am Yisrael. It was a special attention demonstrating God's shining countenance toward Israel. This is the essence of the celebration.

A story is told of a family reunion during which the family patriarch showed for the first time an ancient diamond of incomparable beauty. It was also priceless. In the midst of the excitement and admiration, the diamond disappeared as it was being passed from one hand to another. A tense atmosphere replaced the family's festive mood. With determination, everyone searched for the precious stone, when a child's sudden cry broke the worrisome silence. To everyone's relief, he had found the diamond. The child's pride was compounded when, under the envious glare of all, the patriarch walked to him with a hug and a kiss.

Likewise, the miracle of the small flask of oil represented God's *ha'arat panim*, favorable disposition toward Am Yisrael. It was the additional embrace and kiss.

When Joseph was sold by his brothers to a caravan of Ishmaelites, he was privy to a divine miracle.[14] Usually, the Ishmaelite traders carry on their camels' back cattle hides of unpleasant odors. But this particular caravan carried balsam, spices and lotus.[15] God intervened so that the righteous Joseph would be exposed to pleasant fragrances during the long journey to Egypt. Again, this divine intervention seems completely futile,

14 *Yalkut Shimoni*, Bereshit, 247

15 Genesis, 37:25

considering the sudden tragedy that had just befallen Joseph. Being cut off at a young age from his father with whom he was learning Torah, and driven to a land of immorality as a slave with no chance of freedom, how does this seemingly insignificant miracle play into the whole scheme of things? Granted, it is a small gesture, but its importance is immeasurable. At a time when Joseph's world was crumbling around him, when there seems to be no hope, God sends Joseph a signal that He is behind all these troublesome events and that Joseph has no reason to fall into depression. Just as with the miracle of the oil, the fragrant spices represent God's *ha'arat panim* with Joseph. He should not feel abandoned; rather, Joseph should experience God's *hashgacha pratit*, constant control over all events.

Similarly, when David confronted Goliath and struck him on his forehead, Goliath's body collapsed and fell on his face: "and [David] struck the Philistine in the forehead. The stone penetrated his forehead, and he fell upon his face, upon the ground."[16] The laws of physics call for Goliath's body to fall backward as he was struck on his forehead, how did he fall upon his face? As Goliath was thirteen feet high, God wanted to spare David from walking twenty-six feet toward Goliath's head which David cut off. Again, this divine intervention is of no consequence when we consider the humiliating defeat of the Philistines and the great salvation gained by Israel. Yet, this action is also part of God's *ha'arat panim* toward those He cherishes.

Now we better appreciate the value of the flask of oil. The object of that miracle consisted in conveying to Am Yisrael a greater message, that of God's love for them, it is His *ha'arat panim*, gracious countenance, a divine embrace and kiss to His people. ■

The Victory of the Oral Law

Throughout the period of the First Temple, God's presence was clearly revealed to the Jewish People. He had the prophets guide them in the same manner that He had them led in the Wilderness under the leadership of

16 I Samuel 17:49

Moses.[17] This period concluded with the last prophecy calling on Israel to rely from that point on the Sages' teachings, and informing them that there would be no more prophets until the return of Elijah: "Remember the Torah of Moses My servant, which I commanded him at Horeb for all of Israel – its decrees and its statutes. Behold, I send you Elijah the prophet before the coming of the great and awesome day of Hashem."[18]

However, during the Second Temple, the divine gift of prophecy had ceased, and God interacted with the Jewish People through the Sages of each generation who meticulously transmitted the Oral Law. The Temple stood thanks to the merits of the Torah scholars who lived in Israel and in Babylon. The interaction was achieved solely through the Oral Law.

The Oral Torah is the *neshama* of the Written Torah. The latter, being of higher spiritual status, can be written upon a parchment, a physical entity. For, the higher the spirituality of an article, the more it is susceptible to experience a lower transformation into a materialistic representation such as a parchment. On the other hand, the Oral Law is verbally transmitted by the Sages of each generation.

At the Creation of the world, God created His Glorious Throne along with the souls of the righteous hewed beneath it. He also created the Oral Torah that is embedded within these souls.[19] As a condition to Creation, God consulted these souls and inquired as to their readiness to observe the Oral Torah. The holiness of the Oral Law necessitates that it should not be written, since it is embedded within the souls of the righteous. Their spiritual status will be affected if this Torah is put into writing.

Since the souls of the righteous are hewed beneath God's Glorious Throne, and considering that their holiness derives from the Oral Torah, the latter defines the separation between Israel and the nations of the world.

---

17 R. Sherer, *Ohr Gedaliahu*, Jerusalem: 1990, Chanukah,1-4

18 Malachi 3:22

19 *Sefer HaMabit*, Introduction

It is a fact that the nations' sciences do not tolerate contradictions. However, notwithstanding the opposing opinions encountered within the Oral Law, such as when one Sage issues a *halachic* ruling in contrast to a ruling issued by another Sage on the same topic, they all originate from the One same Shepherd:[20] "God spoke all these statements."[21] In the same manner that many opposing elements, such as fire and water, originated from One Creator, we hold that all the seemingly contradicting opinions of the Sages come from One Source. There is complete unity in the upper spheres. We proclaim that a set of opinions along with the opposing set of ideas originate from One Living God. This concept equally applies to the Sages' *takkanot* – decrees and rabbinical ordinances.

As an example, we find in the Talmud that in the towns that came under the religious jurisdiction of Rabbi Eliezer, people chopped wood on Shabbat in contradiction to the Sages' opinion, until the time when Rabbi Eliezer's ruling was no longer upheld.[22] There is only One Source to the differing rulings and it was a manifestation of the Divine Will that until such a period, the populace in those geographic areas would chop wood on Shabbat according to a specific path of logic built in the Torah. What appeared to be a contradiction was in reality fully reconciled in the heavenly spheres.

The First Temple stood and lasted as long as it did thanks to the merits of the three Patriarchs, Abraham, Isaac and Jacob, who were the antidotes to the three cardinal sins, namely idol worship, prohibited conjugal relations and the spilling of innocent blood. The First Temple was destroyed when the Jews committed these three sins.

The Second Temple stood on the merit of *Knesset Yisrael*, that is, thanks to the holiness of the Oral Torah which the Sages studied and taught. Once unjustifiable hatred settled inside their individual souls, then, *Knesset Yisrael* – literally the gathering of Israel – could no longer hold together, leading to the fall of the Second Temple. Slander caused a schism within *Knesset Yisrael* and weakened the chain of the Sages' authority.

---

20 BT *Chagigah* 3b

21 Exodus 20:1

22 BT *Shabbat* 130a

At the dawn of the Second Temple period, since prophecy was no longer on hand, the Sages eliminated through their prayers the human desire to worship idols.[23] It is because the divine reward for conquering idol worship is prophecy.[24] This explains why false prophets and idol worship were prevalent during the times of the First Temple. These forces countered the gift of prophecy. However, during the Second Temple, the interaction between God and Am Yisrael was essentially based on the Sages' Oral teachings, rather than on prophecy – an assertion of the Written Torah – so the inclination toward idol worship during that period was eliminated. This is in line with the principle of "*zeh le'umat zeh assah Elokim*" – "God has created within each individual opposing forces of comparable influence to counter each other." The gift of prophecy was proportionate to the inclination toward idol worship. When prophecy disappeared, idol worshipping within the Land of Israel ceased.

However, this development creates an inconsistency with regard to Moses's request of God: "and I and Your people will be made distinct from every people on the face of the earth!"[25] Rashi explains that Moses prayed that God would not grant prophecy to any other nation except to Israel, and through this distinction they would remain different from all other nations. How was Moses's request fulfilled during the Second Temple when prophecy ceased? At that time, a lower level of prophecy was granted to the Sages thanks to the piercing logic and wisdom of the Oral Torah. This is *Ruach HaKodesh*, generally translated as the Holy Spirit, where God still relayed His messages to the Sages, albeit in a less overt fashion as prophecy. As the nations cannot relate to the Oral Torah, only the Jews will benefit from *Ruach HaKodesh*. Then, the distinction between the Jewish People and other nations is still maintained.

This was the heinous goal that the Hellenists sought to achieve. They wanted to remove this distinction by polluting the souls of Am Yisrael with alien philosophies. Just as prophecy is opposed by the forces of idol worshipping, the Oral Torah is weakened by foreign ideologies. Hellenism stood in flagrant contradiction to the Sages' Torah. The Greeks' culture sought to eliminate the Oral Law.

---

23 BT *Yomah* 69b

24 The Gaon of Vilna, *Hagahot Seder Olam*

25 Exodus 33:16

Inside the Temple were two vessels of the highest significance. The Ark contained the Testimonial-tablets representing the Written Torah, and the Menorah of pure gold whose lights symbolized the Oral Torah. Under the leadership of Moses, the first Sanctuary was built in the Wilderness because God wanted to dwell in the midst of Am Yisrael in the same way His presence descended upon Mount Sinai.[26] So for forty years, both aspects of the Torah – the written and the oral – flourished through two faithful emissaries: Moses and Aaron, the High Priest. For forty years, Aaron was in charge of lighting the Menorah every day, symbolizing man's personal efforts and intellectual pursuits to understanding and upholding the Oral Law. It is through the Menorah lights, representing the Oral Torah, that God grants the Sages the authority to issue additional ordinances or decrees. Is God not the light to the entire universe? Why does He ask the High Priest to light a few more flames? It is God's desire to dwell in the midst of Israel, and because He eagerly awaits the deeds of the righteous – symbolized by the lights of Chanukah – to trigger the flow of divine blessings upon the world.

In addition to the miracle of the military battle of Chanukah, there was also a spiritual struggle – to see that the Oral Torah would overcome the Greek culture. That is the reason the miracle of Chanukah revolves around the lights of the Menorah which represent the Oral Law. It is an everlasting victory by the Torah Sages against the darkness of alien ideologies. ■

THE HASMONEANS CONTINUE THE LEGACY OF AARON, THE HIGH PRIEST

The lights of the Menorah symbolizing the Oral Torah were first lit in the Tabernacle by Aaron, the High Priest. Many years later, His descendants, the Hasmoneans who fought the Greeks, lit the lights of Chanukah. In doing so, says the Arizal, they performed a *tikkun* to the *Sefirah Hod* (splendor), which equally corresponds to the Oral Torah. The splendor of an individual is underlined by the personal efforts he invests in his spiritual growth and in the amelioration of his character traits. Likewise, the Oral Torah calls on the Jew to take the initiative and increment his

26 Ramban, introduction to Terumah

service of God. The *Sefirah Hod* represents the personal aspirations and endeavors to reach higher spiritual levels.[27] So our Sages link the Beit Hamikdash to the *Sefirah Hod* because, through the intermediary of the Temple, God's presence in our midst is justified, as He awaits our active devotion which, in turn, triggers a flow of divine blessings.[28] Thus all the rituals inside the Beit Hamikdash are called *avodah*, work, referring to man's effort in worshipping God. So the Temple which corresponds to the *Sefirah Hod* is the right place for the priest's service of God. By restoring the rituals to the Beit Hamikdash, the Hasmoneans achieved a *tikkun* to the attribute of splendor.

As the descendants of Japheth (which also translates into beauty), the Greeks sought to deprive the *Sefirah Hod* from its internal splendor and impose on the Jewish People the glorification of the strong and the vain. "May God extend Japheth, but He will dwell in the tents of Shem [the father of the Jewish nation]."[29] External beauty has value only when internal beauty is also present. The Greeks glorified the strong and chose to ignore what the tents of Shem stood for – reverence of God.

Our Sages teach that all is under God's control save for the reverence of God.[30] The fear of God lies with man's choice, a personal effort. As with the *Sefirah Hod*, the fear of God necessitates that man adopts an active path for worshipping God, which really is the attribute of the priests inside the Temple. As Aaron's descendants, the Hasmoneans lived up to the characteristics of the attribute of *Hod*, and had the merit to purify the Temple. Thanks to their victory, they restored the internal splendor of the *Sefirah Hod* which is linked to the Oral Torah, the embodiment of man's individual efforts. ■

ACTIVE PARTICIPANTS IN THE MIRACLE

In his book, *War of the Jews*, Josephus Flavius (Yosef Ben Matityahu), describes the Hasmoneans as strong and audacious warriors. Indeed, it

---

27 R. Sherer *Ohr Gedaliahu*, Chanukah, 5

28 BT *Brachot* 58a

29 Genesis 9:27

30 BT *Brachot* 33b

takes a lot of courage to go into battle with the untrained few against the many who had conquered and subdued several nations. Yet, the passage we add to the daily services during Chanukah refers to them as feeble: "In Your great compassion Hashem, You stood up for them in their time of trouble, and delivered the strong into the hands of the weak."

The Exodus from Egypt was an irrefutable proof of God's intervention on behalf of Israel. The extraction of an entire nation from Egypt introduced to mankind God's unlimited powers.[31] Likewise, under the threat of annihilation by Haman, God saved Israel. However, under the Hellenists' threat, the Jews physically fought the enemy. As the Hasmoneans were righteous, they were afraid of falling into the common trap of taking credit for their prowess and uniquely relying on their battle tactics. They went to war while witnessing God's miracles unravel in front of their eyes. They understood that when an individual is personally involved in a military victory, the challenge of attributing all victories only to God is even greater. It is far easier to claim that the outcome resulted from personal strength. Instead, righteous as they were, the Hasmoneans attributed the military triumph to God's assistance. In this sense, they mentally wore the "mantle of weakness," asserting that their victory was completely willed by God.

Consequently, the Hasmoneans deserved the merit of the oil's miracle. The flask which should have lasted one day lit for eight days. The lit candles reflected the Hasmoneans dignified introspection of the war's conclusion. The victory came from God. Thus a strong bond exists between the miracle of the lights of Chanukah and the salvation of Am Yisrael. Both events point at the noble self-examination and humility of the Hasmoneans. Ever since, Jews all over the world stare at the Chanukah flames with a humble heart and gratitude to God. Today, these lights continue to inspire us to examine our relationship with God.

Moments before lighting, a blessing is uttered in which we thank God for performing miracles on behalf of our forefathers "*bayamim hahem bazeman hazeh*" – "in those days, at this time." The same is recited at the reading of the Megillah on Purim. However, this blessing is not read

---

31 R. Levy Yitzhak of Berditchev, *Kedushat Levy*, Chanukah

at all when we recall the Exodus from Egypt or the crossing of the Red Sea, because these last events were markedly above the laws of nature. The divine involvement to save the Jews simply flowed from heaven. However, on Chanukah and Purim, the Hasmoneans and Queen Esther were active participants in the miracle which they experienced. To this day, the Chanukah miracle remains an integral part of our world. As the radiating Divine Light which willed it is renewed on the 25th of Kislev each year, it is a propitious time to benefit from divine kindness. We highlight this phenomenon with the emphasis on "*bayamim hahem bazeman hazeh*." As we light a total of thirty-six lights during the eight days, thirty-six more lights are lit in heaven in a reciprocating manner. This brings the total to seventy-two lights and corresponds to the numerical value of the divine name *yud keh vav keh* (when it is fully spelled). This is a testimony to God's unwavering interest in the People of Israel.

Thus the mystical flames of Chanukah that we set off in heaven, reflect our commitment to spiritual aspirations symbolized by our own lights. This translates into the idea of *it'aruta dil'teitah*, where man, through his actions, initiates God's response. In many instances, as when God saved the Jewish People from Egypt, the initiative was purely His. In those situations, even when the Jews are undeserving, God steps in to save them, because of His love for them. But, in most instances, our relationship with God necessitates that we trigger the *it'aruta dil'teitah*, the awakening call. Just as the commotion of a shadow reflects the body's movements, so do heaven's reactions reflect man's behavior. When he acts with kindness, he is dealt with kindness; when he acts with cruelty, the heavenly response mirrors his conduct. Man is urged to emulate his Creator's attributes of forgiveness, generosity and compassion. By doing so, man will be the ultimate winner.

The miracle of Chanukah saw the intense participation of the Hasmoneans who are Levites, while other historical events were performed by the leaders of the tribe of Judah. (Although the Hasmoneans are Kohanim, they belong to the tribe of Levi.) This distinction follows the mystical association present within the four natural elements and the first four tribes begotten by Leah, our Matriarch. Corresponding to Reuben's tribe is water which represents the divine flow of abundance. Shimon relates to fire which invokes *tzimzum*, limitation of the divine abundance. The Levites are linked to the wind, symbolizing the intermediary forces between abundance and constraint. Judah represents *Knesset Yisrael*, the Jewish People, about whom it is written: "I will make your offspring as the dust of the earth..."[32] This explains why Judah steps in whenever a physical threat hangs over Am Yisrael. However, during the Greek tyrannical rule, the menace was mostly spiritual since they aimed at forcing the Jews away from the Torah. It is then the role of the Levites, the Torah guardians, to take the initiative and save the Jewish People. They did so with a humble heart, recalling the exceptional humility of their teacher Moses, who too was a Levite. Indeed, the Torah so testifies: "Now the man Moses was exceedingly humble, more than any person of the earth!"[33] ■

CHANUKAH LIGHTS HIGHLIGHT TORAH EDUCATION

When Jacob ran away from his brother Esau who sought to kill him, he first stopped by Shem's Yeshiva and learned Torah for fourteen years. Jacob reasoned that since he was leaving the Land of Israel for the *galut*, exile, he had to strengthen his spiritual status lest he fails. Since idol worship and immoral mores prevailed in the foreign lands, Jacob readied himself for innumerable challenges by studying Torah.

Likewise, years later, on the way to Egypt to reunite with his son Joseph, Jacob first sent Judah to establish a Torah learning center in Goshen, Egypt. Jacob was convinced that without Torah it is practically impossible to remain a faithful Jew in the *galut*.[34] Thus the Talmud states that our ancestors always maintained a Torah learning program as an antidote to the negative influence of alien cultures.[35]

Similarly, when Alexander Mokdon, the founder of the Greek Empire, met for the first time Shimon HaTzaddik, the last leader of the Great Assembly, he dismounted his horse and, to the dismay of his generals, bowed to him.[36] Alexander explained that the night prior to every

---

32 Genesis 13:16

33 Numbers 12:3

34 R. Nosson Meir Wachtfogel, *Kovetz Sichot*, Vayigash

35 BT *Yomah* 28b

36 BT Ibid., 69a

battle and conquest, he always saw in a dream the holy face of Shimon HaTzaddik, the High Priest. The latter realized the grave dangers posed by this new invasion of the Land of Israel. He used his meeting with Alexander to obtain concessions for the defense of Torah institutes. Shimon HaTzaddik understood that Israel can sail through this new exile only if they remain faithful to the Torah.

Our Sages were unanimous on the only guarantee to the continued existence of the Jewish People in exile. It is a Torah education and methodical Torah study programs. This approach is so vital that the Talmud describes it as more important than the building of the Holy Temple.[37] Ezra the Scribe delayed his departure from Persia to the Holy Land for as long as his rabbi, Baruch Ben Neriah, remained alive. Ezra stayed in exile longer to learn Torah from his master. It is only after Baruch Ben Neriah passed away, that Ezra returned to Jerusalem to spearhead the construction of the Second Temple and to organize the resettlement of the Jews in Israel.

All the nations who persecuted the Jewish People did so to uproot the Torah from them. Regardless of the justifications given, the politics involved, the historical upheavals and revolutions – their main objective was all the same. When Babylon invaded Jerusalem, their main goal was to destroy the Temple, the seat of the Torah. It was not enough that they conquered every world capital, they had to burn down the Temple. Likewise, the Greek yoke was driven by the same objective: "When the evil Greek Empire rose up against Your people, Israel, to cause them to forget Your Torah, and to force them to turn from the statutes of Your Will."[38]

What is the Jewish answer? "You delivered tyrants into the hands of those who are occupied with Your Torah." The study of Torah represents our indispensable survival kit in the *galut*. In fact, a higher level of commitment is expected of us in exile – it is to be occupied with Torah. In the same manner that a farmer is occupied with the daily toil of his farm, and a doctor with the needs of his patients, we too must demonstrate full-time dedication to the Torah.

37 BT *Megillah* 16b

38 *Al Hanissim*, Chanukah prayer

Moreover, the Talmud asks why Chanukah is the last of the recorded miracles.[39] The Sages answer that the self-sacrifice which the Jews demonstrated during that period established the foundation of the forthcoming *galut*.[40] As they struggled to keep the Torah, Chanukah became a staging platform for future generations in exile. In the foreign lands, the Jewish People will maintain their integrity and moral strength only by remaining loyal to the Torah principles.

When Moses and Betzalel built the first Mishkan (Tabernacle) in the Wilderness, it was inaugurated during a period of twelve days. Every day, a different tribe leader offered his inaugural sacrifices. Aaron, the High Priest, felt left out of the inauguration ceremony. God told Moses that Aaron's role in the inauguration will be greater through the Hasmoneans, his descendants. The lights of Chanukah will accompany the Jewish People across their exile under Edom. They will always remind Israel of the underlying message of Chanukah: "You delivered tyrants into the hands of those who are occupied with Your Torah." Being "occupied" with Torah study is the only guarantee to the continuity of Am Yisrael in the *galut*. Although it is better known as the festival of lights, Chanukah is mostly a *yom tov shel Torah* – a Torah celebration.

Moreover, while today's children look forward to receiving Chanukah *gelt*, money, in the past it was actually given as a token of appreciation to Jewish educators. Chanukah is linked to education, with *chinuch* (education) and Chanukah sharing the same root in Hebrew. The light emanating from the Chanukah candles bring to mind that "Torah is light" as King Solomon stated in Proverbs. The rabbis in 18th century Eastern Europe kept the light of Jewish tradition aglow by teaching the children and adults in their communities. During Chanukah, they would leave their towns and travel to outlying villages to teach Torah. This intense study period benefitted the villagers the year round. Initially the rabbis declined pay, so appreciative villagers gave them token gifts or *gelt* until this practice became obligatory. ■

39 BT *Yomah* 29a

40 *Midrash Tanchumah*, Behaalotecha 5

Purim

Purim

The damage that Amalek and his followers are able to accomplish is proportionate to the flaw in Israel's worship of God. The deeper Israel's failing, the greater the desecration achieved by other nations. The more Godliness Israel promotes, the weaker the enemies' ideology becomes. Such is the inextricable idea of imal'ah hachoravah – *when one ideology rises, the other one is destroyed. The power in the hands of evil nations is commensurate to Israel's spiritual failure. The situation where "trembling gripped the powers of Moab," would have continued had Israel kept an implacable attachment to the Torah. Israel's failure at a time when they experienced divine miracles made a lasting mark for generations to come. The* tikkun *will necessitate furthering God's glory through remembering Amalek's designs as well as Israel's spiritual failings. The fall of Amalek is closely knit with Israel's ardent dedication to Torah. Even today, we can safely make this prediction: the boldness of the nations to condemn, threaten or harm Israel is invariably commensurate to Israel's religious commitment.*

YOM KIPPUR IS LIKE PURIM

The Arizal suggests that on Purim one can reach a spiritual experience far greater than on Yom Kippur[1] by living up to the Sages' recommendation, whereby a person must get drunk on Purim to the point where he will not know the difference between cursing Haman and blessing Mordechai.[2] What precisely does the Arizal mean? How is it possible to reach a higher spiritual level on Purim than on the fearful Day of Judgment and atonement?[3]

When King Hezekiah became ill, he was visited by the prophet Isaiah who delivered God's message stating that King Hezekiah's death was imminent: "Isaiah, son of Amoz, the prophet, came to him and said to him: 'Thus said Hashem: Instruct your household, for you shall die; and you shall not live.'"[4] The Talmud explains that a heavenly death sentence was issued against the King of Israel because he chose not to have children.[5] King Hezekiah foresaw through his *Ruach HaKodesh* that he would beget wicked children. So he deliberately chose not to bring children to this world. The prophet rebuked him saying he has no business stepping into God's arena. King Hezekiah deserved such a severe sentence mostly because he offered a justification to exempt himself from a Torah commandment. This act amounts to throwing away the yoke of heaven. When a person relies on his reasoning whether to fulfill a divine commandment or to bypass it, then, essentially, he sets himself free from God's service. Even when the decision is based on noble ideals, it is simply unacceptable. Our role is to abide by God's Will, rather than to evaluate it.

It was along this logic that, following the near sacrifice of Isaac, God complimented Abraham: "for now I know that you are a God-fearing man."[6] Abraham ignored all rational justifications and went ahead to fulfill God's command. He did so, knowing this sacrifice contradicted God's

---

1 *Shelah Hakadosh*, Tetsaveh, 2
2 BT *Meggilah* 7b
3 R. Chaim Shmuelevitz *Sichot Mussar* 52
4 II Kings 20:1
5 *Brachot* 10a
6 Genesis 22:12

early promise to build the Jewish nation from Isaac. He did not question God's wish and proceeded to sacrifice his son, an act which defied the principles of kindness he upheld and preached all his life.

The greatness that one can achieve on Purim consists in worshipping God without personal calculations to the point where he will not "distinguish between cursing Haman and blessing Mordechai." The true *eved Hashem*, God's servant, should acknowledge the Torah commandments along with rabbinical ordinances, because they are issued by God.[7] We must not allow our personal preferences or logic supersede the divine dictates.

Likewise, when King Saul failed in his mission to wipe out Amalek, he too was severely punished as he lost the Kingship of Israel. He was informed of his demise by the prophet Samuel: "For rebelliousness is like the sin of sorcery and verbosity is like the iniquity of idolatry. Because you have rejected the word of God, He has rejected you as king!"[8] Samuel told Saul that verbose rationalizations are as empty as the extravagant rituals of idol worship, and they are no substitute for obedience to God. King Saul's castigation resulted not so much because he did not fully carry his mission, but because he attempted to justify his conduct. God treats such behavior as shaking away the heavenly yoke. On the other hand, King David's sin was forgiven because it was viewed as a general failure rather than a rejection of God's yoke.[9]

Similarly, in the full fury of the destruction of the First Temple and of Jerusalem, the prophet Ezekiel reveals a vision (similar to the earlier *Merkavah* vision, where Ezekiel speaks of the workings of the Heavenly Throne, a topic which is far removed from human comprehension) of what took place at that tragic time around the Divine Throne: "The Cherub stretched out his hand from between the Cherubim to the fire that was between the Cherubim, and he carried [the fire] and put it into the cupped hands of the one clothed in linen [the angel Gabriel]."[10]

---

7 Deuteronomy 17:11. "You shall not deviate from the word that they [rabbis] will tell you." This too is a Torah imperative.

8 I Samuel 15:23

9 BT *Yomah* 22b

10 Ezekiel 10:7

God had commanded the angel Gabriel to take the blazing fire from the proximity of the Cherubim and destroy the city. Instead, the angel Gabriel asked another angel to bring him the fire. In doing so, the blazing fire cooled down somehow, thus avoiding a complete annihilation of Am Yisrael. (We must relate to this vision within a spiritual concept). Says Rabbi Yochanan, at that moment the angel Gabriel was taken aside and given sixty fiery lashes for disobeying God's command.[11] As he sought to mitigate the full destruction of the city, he used the intermediate services of another angel instead of taking the fire himself as he was commanded. The heavenly court punished the angel Gabriel for carrying God's command with reservations and justifications. Notwithstanding his noble cause to spare Am Yisrael, the angel Gabriel's action is viewed as a rejection of God's yoke.

In fulfilling a rabbinical teaching to drink wine on Purim – *ad d'lo yadah*, to the point where one would not recognize the difference between a curse to Haman, Israel's enemy, and a blessing to Mordechai – and readily dismiss our intellectual objection to such an ordinance, we, says the Arizal, can reach spiritual levels higher than on Yom Kippur. Through this approach, one can live the true definition of *eved Hashem*. ■

Our Perpetual War against Amalek

Amalek, the embodiment of evil on earth, treacherously attacked the Jews soon after they left the Egyptian bondage.[12] The sudden assault targeted more their belief and less their body. The newly formed nation carried a ray of hope for mankind through monotheism, in the form of respect for human life and social justice. This was too much for Amalek who sought to subjugate by the sword. As this battle of ideologies unraveled, Moses prayed for a favorable outcome: "Moses's hands grew heavy, so they took a stone and put it under him, and he sat on it, and Aaron and Hur supported his hands... and he remained with his hands in faithful prayer until sunset."[13]

11 BT *Yomah* 77a

12 Rabbinical tradition holds that Haman descended from Amalek.

13 Exodus 17:12

First, what makes Moses's hands heavy?[14] Second, how do we understand the concept of "faithful hands?" Additionally, why is this war against Amalek described as a difficult war, more so than any other war? In fact, it was a daunting war, as it says: "Hashem maintains a war against Amalek from generation to generation."[15]

Also, there is the famous Talmudic question, "Could it be that the position of Moses's hands would determine the outcome of the battle?" Rather, answers the Talmud: "when the Jews raise their heart toward God, then they are victorious; otherwise, they are vanquished."[16] How could such a dramatic change of heart take place in one day? In the Zohar, Rabbi Shimon bar Yochai explains that the war against Amalek was particularly difficult because it took place in Heaven as well as down on earth. The ideology of Amalek, the forces of impurity, consisted of uprooting from the hearts of Am Yisrael the main ingredient of their relationship with God — their *emunah*.

The struggle took place in Heaven because God created both good and evil. With the Jewish People readying itself to accept and live by the Torah as a nation, the time for good to strongly assert itself had come. The evil, represented by the forces of Amalek, was striving to sow into the minds of Israel seeds of doubt and suspicion concerning the truthfulness of God, of the Torah, and of Moses. Hence, as soon as the children of Israel questioned God's ability to provide for them while in the desert, their enemy Amalek appeared in order to deepen that doubt in their hearts and remove every kernel of faith, God forbid.

Similarly, our Sages hold that the strength of Moses rested with his power to instill soundly into the minds of Am Yisrael faith in God. Therefore, when Moses read the evil intent of Amalek, the atheist, he called on Joshua to handpick an army of righteous men. At the same time, Moses encouraged Am Yisrael to maintain their faith in God, as an antidote and challenge to Amalek. When Moses raised his hands, he was successful in strengthening the *emunah* of the Jewish People, and they were victorious.

14 *Maor Vashemesh*, Exodus 17:12

15 Exodus 17:16

16 BT *Rosh Hashana* 29a

But when the seeds of doubt overtook the hearts of the children of Israel, the ideology of Amalek to uproot their faith became stronger.

Consequently, the hands of Moses felt heavy. Yet, Moses pursued his objective of instilling into Israel's heart unquestionable faith in God. As a result of his spiritual leadership, Joshua weakened Amalek and its people by the sword's blade. However, in spite of that historical defeat of Amalek, its reprehensible philosophy affected many, who to this day err after false pursuits. As a result, God maintains a war against Amalek from generation to generation until the arrival of our righteous Mashiach. At that time, belief in the God of Israel will spread throughout the entire world. ■

God Concealed His Face from Israel

The idea of God's concealment from Bnei Yisrael is conveyed in the Torah: "Hashem said to Moses, Behold, you will lie with your forefathers, but this people will rise up and stray after the gods of the foreigners of the land, in whose midst it is coming... My anger will flare against it on that day... But I will surely have concealed My face [*haster aster*] on that day... So now, write this song for yourselves, and teach it to the Children of Israel..."[17]

Our Sages hold that the frightening episode of Haman and his evil decrees against the Jewish nation were hinted at in the verse above.[18] God's concealment from mankind, which is highlighted by the name Esther, the heroine of the Purim story, invariably results in a period of darkness and human calamities. In the holy book of the Zohar, Rabbi Shimon bar Yochai suggests that the Children of Israel who returned from Babylon to Eretz Yisrael at the end of their first exile should have witnessed miracles as great as those performed by God during the Exodus from Egypt. However, due to the sin of intermarriage with the Babylonian women, the Jews were unworthy of the divine manifestation. The sin of the *brit*, notes the Zohar, brings the worst blemish onto the Jewish People and causes a schism with God. In contrast, during Am Yisrael's stay in Egypt, despite adverse conditions, they meticulously guarded the holiness of the *brit*,

17 Deuteronomy 31:16-19
18 R. Yaakov Abuchatzeira, *Pituchei Chotam*, Vayelech 31:16

the purity of marital relations. As a result, Bnei Yisrael deserved to see God's miracles. In Babylon, the Jewish People forfeited what would have been a grandiose return to their land, because they married alien women.

As a result of the concealment of the divine protection, Haman was emboldened to issue threatening decrees, which were canceled thanks to the righteousness of Mordechai and Esther. In fact, the numerical value of מרדכי, 274, is equal to that of "קם העם הזה" – "this people will rise up" (272 plus 2 for the two words קם העם), mentioned in the context of divine concealment which will occur during the story of Purim. It is a hint in the Torah of Mordechai's merit, who will draw strength from the everlasting spiritual greatness of Moses. Our Sages explain that "he will rise up," in the future tense, refers to Moses's merits, which will give vigor and spiritual support to Mordechai later in history.

Haman understood that nothing could drive a powerful wedge between Am Yisrael and their God as their failure to maintain the holiness of the *brit*. Such failure would weaken the love that exists between God and the Jewish People, and then they would become vulnerable to assault by external enemies such as Haman without divine protection. When Haman saw that Bnei Yisrael were intermarrying, he was confident that the unique relationship between the Jews and their God would dissipate. This encouraged Haman to issue his dreadful decrees. However, his evil schemes were defeated thanks to the merits of Esther, also implied in the word *haster*, conceal. In His infinite kindness, God offered a way out: "So now, write this song." The way to the *tikkun* of the failure of the *brit* was to write and learn the Torah. It would act as atonement for the Jewish People and would reinstate the everlasting love of God toward His people. This is implied in the text of the Megillah: "The Jews had gladness" where gladness is a reference to Torah which reinforces the unique bond between God and Israel. ■

AMALEK SINGLED OUT FROM OTHER NATIONS

"For the hand is on the Throne of God: Hashem maintains a war against Amalek, from generation to generation."[19] With these words, the

19 Exodus 17:16

Torah urges the Jewish People to remain vigilant against Amalek and the forces of evil which that nation embodies.[20] We are commanded to remember the treacherous attack which Amalek launched against the newly formed nation of Israel soon after they left the Egyptian bondage. At that time, all other nations had heard of God's intervention on behalf of Israel. The Ten Plagues which brought utter destruction upon Egypt, and the drowning of the Egyptian army at the Red Sea left the mighty generals of the surrounding nations awed and fearful: "Peoples heard – they were agitated: terror gripped the dwellers of Philistia. Then the chieftains of Edom were confounded, trembling gripped the powers of Moab, all the dwellers of Canaan dissolved."[21] No nation dared attack Israel until Amalek, Esau's descendant, stepped in and broke the fear that gripped all nations. In doing so, he breached a silent agreement and invited all nations to follow suit and persecute the Jews.

As Amalek represents the forces of evil, Israel's war against him is equally eternal. It is so because his deliberate defiance of Godliness diminishes God's glory in the world. It becomes Israel's role to defeat Amalek's destructive ideology and elevate God's Name around the world. This struggle continues from generation to generation until the advent of Mashiach when God's Name will be glorified throughout the world.

Moreover, whenever the Jewish People is saved through a divine miracle, Israel's tormentors are struck. The retributions which befell Pharaoh, Sancheriv and Haman reinforce the process toward the final redemption. It is so because with the fall of evil comes a greater recognition of Godliness. Any divine intervention which strikes evil-doers promotes the concept of divine justice and reminds mankind that this world is not ownerless.

The constant battle between good and evil is further emphasized with the Sages' commentary on the prophet's words:[22] "Son of Man: Because Tyre has said of Jerusalem, 'Hurrah! The gateways of the nations have been broken; it is turned toward me! I will be filled, for she

20 R. Kotler, *Mishnat Rabbi Aharon*, III, Purim

21 Exodus !5:14

22 BT *Megillah* 6a

was destroyed!'"[23] Says the Talmud: "Should anyone announce the simultaneous destruction of Jerusalem and Rome, ignore him. If you are told that Jerusalem and Rome have been rebuilt, you should know it is a lie. But if you are told one of these places has fallen and the other has risen, then, you should believe it." Both cities, along with the opposing ideologies they represent, cannot thrive at the same time. It is the concept of *imal'ah hachoravah* – when one ideology rises, the other one is destroyed. When God's glory is manifest, evil is beaten down. And when evil has the upper hand, Godliness is debased. As Amalek intentionally rebels against God, Am Yisrael is commanded to perpetuate the fight against evil and promote Godliness in the world. The more we enhance God's glory the more we contribute to wiping out the memory of Amalek.

"Remember what Amalek did to you, on the way when you were leaving Egypt…"[24] We clearly see that it is a Torah commandment to verbally recall Amalek's attack. It is performed once a year, on the Shabbat preceding Purim, by reading the Torah portion dealing with this episode. In reality, the other underlying message rests with the cause that brought this catastrophe upon Israel. It is, says the Midrash, the Jews' weak commitment to Torah:[25] "Amalek came and battled Israel in Rephidim."[26] The Hebrew translation for Rephidim implies weakness. Am Yisrael did not abandon the Torah. Rather, they approached it with a lack of enthusiasm and in a detached manner. Thus God's rebuke is veiled. By remembering Amalek's attack, they should recall what triggered this war.

The damage that Amalek and his followers are able to accomplish is proportionate to the flaw in Israel's worship of God. The deeper Israel's failing, the greater the desecration achieved by other nations. The more Godliness Israel promotes, the weaker the enemies' ideology becomes. Such is the inextricable idea of *imal'ah hachoravah*. The power in the hands of evil nations is commensurate to Israel's spiritual failure. The situation where "trembling gripped the powers of Moab" would have continued had Israel kept an implacable attachment to the Torah. Israel's failure at a time when they experienced divine miracles made a lasting mark for

23 Ezekiel 26:2

24 Deuteronomy 25:11

25 *Tanchumah*, Beshalach 25

26 Exodus 17:8

generations to come. The *tikkun* will necessitate furthering God's glory through remembering Amalek's designs as well as Israel's spiritual failings. The fall of Amalek is closely knit with Israel's ardent dedication to Torah.

Even today, we can safely make this prediction: the boldness of the nations to condemn, threaten or harm Israel is invariably commensurate to Israel's religious commitment. ■

MORDECHAI'S AURA OF SILENCE AND POWER OF SPEECH

The book relating the miracle of Purim is commonly known as *Megillat Esther*. Mordechai is introduced there as "*ish Yemini*," a descendant from the tribe of Benjamin. He is equally described as "*ish Yehudi*," a descendant from the tribe of Judah. The Sefat Emet explains that Mordechai's lineage goes all the way back to Rachel and Leah who respectively begot Benjamin and Judah.[27] Consequently from his father's side, Mordechai inherited the defining character trait of Rachel and Benjamin – namely silence. Indeed, Benjamin knew that his brothers had sold Joseph as a slave and he never divulged their sinister scheme to his father Jacob. He remained silent to avoid embarrassing his brothers. Likewise, Rachel knew that Laban was to dupe Jacob and offer him Leah as a bride after seven years of labor for Rachel, and she remained silent in front of that treachery. To avoid great embarrassment to her sister, Rachel kept silent.

At the same time, Mordechai inherited the significant character trait of Leah and Judah, namely the ability to say the right words at the right moment. Indeed, when Leah gave birth to her son Judah, she praised God: "This time let me gratefully praise Hashem; therefore she called his name Judah [Yehudah means praise]."[28] In the episode involving Tamar and Judah, the latter declared: "She is right; it is from me, inasmuch I did not give her to Shelah my son." Judah demonstrated his character strength when he acknowledged the truth. As to Leah, she used her faculty of speech to praise Hashem and to express her gratitude.

So, when Haman's decree to annihilate all the Jews in the Persian Empire was released, Mordechai, the *yehudi,* spoke and vehemently implored

27 Sefat Emet, Purim 5648

28 Genesis 29:35

a reluctant Esther to intercede on behalf of her people: "Do not imagine in your soul that you will be able to escape in the king's palace any more than the rest of the Jews... And who knows whether it was just for such a time as this that you attained the royal position!"[29] Mordechai emulated Judah in defending Am Yisrael. On the other hand, when Esther was taken into the King's palace, Mordechai recommended that she not divulge her royal lineage as they both descended from King Saul: "Esther still told nothing of her kindred or her people as Mordechai had instructed her."[30]

The Talmud asks where do we find a hint to Haman in the Torah?[31] It answers by citing the rebuke God delivered to Adam after he sinned: "*Hamin* [*haman*] *ha'etz*, have you eaten of the tree from which I commanded you not to eat?" Why are the Sages interested in finding a hint to Haman in the Torah? Besides, what is the correlation between Haman and the question beginning with *hamin* which the Sages choose to read as Haman?

Rabbi Chaim Vital, the famed disciple of the Arizal, explains that Esther was the reincarnation of Eve.[32] The latter fell to the temptations of the serpent because she did not keep silent when he opened a conversation with her: "He [the serpent] said to the woman, 'Did perhaps God say: "You shall not eat of any tree of the garden?"' The woman said to the serpent, 'Of the fruit of any tree of the garden we may eat. Of the fruit of the tree which is in the center of the garden God has said: "You shall neither eat of it nor touch it, lest you die."'"[33] In fact, God has never issued a warning against touching the Forbidden Tree. Had Eve remained silent, she would not have fallen prey to the snare laid by the serpent. Now, a *tikkun* to Eve's failure can be achieved, to a certain extent, by Esther's attribute of silence.

Since the Jews partook in the forbidden meal and wine offered by King Ahasuerus, they reignited the power of the same primordial serpent that caused Eve's demise to prosecute against the Jews of Persia. So, when the Talmudic Sages looked for a hint to Haman in the Torah, they attempted

29 Esther 4:14

30 Ibid., 2:20

31 BT *Chulin* 139b

32 Bnei Yissachar, Adar 7:9

33 Genesis 3:1-3

to find the reason for the near tragic decree which befell the Jews. It is their participation in a festive meal during Ahasuerus's extravagant celebration. In order to counterbalance the forces of the *yetzer*, the Jews of Persia needed the two leaders who descended from Rachel and Leah and maintained the aura of silence and the value of speech in its propitious time.

The Talmud teaches that just as voice is beneficial to the plants, silence is good for the wine to acquire a better flavor.[34] Thus, the Sages instituted a blessing over the wine at the onset of Shabbat to remind us that in the same manner that silence is good for the wine, so we too must avoid weekday speech on Shabbat. Such is the prophet's injunction: "and you honor it [Shabbat] by not engaging in your own affairs, from seeking your own needs or discussing the forbidden."[35] On Shabbat, one must not address topics discussed during weekdays. So when we consecrate Shabbat by a blessing over the wine, we are invited to keep away from ordinary workday speech. The same rational applies to the blessing recited over the wine at the conclusion of Shabbat. Now that Shabbat is over, we must not give free rein to our tongue during the next weekdays, rather, we must carefully guard our speech. At the same time, we recite a blessing over a plant with good fragrance to symbolize the benefit of speech to the plants. In extolling the virtues of silence, one must know when to speak up. This is the reason Purim's celebration is defined as "days of drinking and gladness," because these are the days in which the Jews gained relief from their enemies.[36] It mostly reminds us of Mordechai's character traits inherited from Rachel and Leah: the power of silence – hinted at in the days of drinking, for silence is beneficial to wine together with the dominant virtue of speech at the right time.

Silence's significance is highlighted by the teachings of Rabbi Shimon ben Gamliel: "All my days I have been raised among the Sages and I found nothing better for oneself than silence, not study, but practice is the main thing, and one who talks excessively brings on sin."[37] Likewise, warning against futile speech, King Solomon writes: "In an abundance of words offense will not be lacking, but one who restrains his lips is wise."[38]

34 BT *Keritut* 6b
35 Isaiah 58:13
36 Esther 9:22
37 *Avot* 1:17
38 Proverbs 10:19

The miracle of Purim is more than a joyous celebration. Being intimately associated with Mordechai and Esther, Purim is a time to reassess God's unique gift to mankind; the faculty of speech. At the propitious time, it must be used to praise God, to express our gratitude and to stand up for the truth and the values of the Torah. Purim equally celebrates the power of silence as represented by *yom mishteh*, a day of wine consumption, for the Talmud in Tractate Shabbat teaches: "*Ein haolam mitkayem ela al mi shebolem piv*" – "the world's existence rests upon those who remain silent in front of insults." ■

WIPING OUT AMALEK THROUGH UNITY

There is a divine commandment to wipe out the memory of Amalek from under the heavens. However, although our Torah is eternal and must be observed daily, how can we be expected to fulfill this commandment when we are in exile under the rule of various powers?[39] To answer this question, we shall first revisit a Mishna: "The reading of the Megillah of Purim takes place on the eleventh of the month of Adar, on the twelfth, the thirteenth, the fourteenth, and the fifteenth, not less or more."[40] The conclusion of this Mishna ought to read "not earlier or later." Rather, it ends with an unusual note: "not less or more."

Our Sages hold that the main pursuit of the Jewish nation should be to achieve solidarity and love. When unity prevails in their ranks, even the worshipping of idols, God forbid, is looked upon in Heaven with indulgence. Such is the learning the Sages derive from the words of God to the prophet Hoshea: "Ephraim is attached to idols; let him be."[41] Due to the unity among the tribes of Israel, then ruled by Ephraim, God overlooked their idolatry, a cardinal sin. Hatred, on the other hand, has proven to be the driving cause of the destruction of the Second Temple along with the prolongation of the current exile.

Furthermore, the harsh heavenly judgments are canceled when love for each other permeates our society. The numerical value of *ahavah*,

39 *Maor Vashemesh*, Exodus 28:32

40 BT *Megillah* 2a

41 Hoshea 4:17

love, equals that of *echad*, one, which is 13, corresponding to the thirteen mystical *tikkunim* which the *tzaddik* draws from a Heavenly source known as the "upper *mazal*." According to the Arizal, when punctuated in a unique way, the word *ahavah* represents one of God's ineffable names.

Commenting on the harm Amalek caused to Israel when they were attacked in the desert, the Midrash translates the verse "*asher karekha*" – "that he happened upon you on the way," to signify a cooling off, as in *kar*, cold.[42] Amalek's prime character trait is conceit. In fact, the numerical value of *kar* is the same as that of *rahm*, haughty. He brought his profane doctrine into the ranks of Am Yisrael and cooled off the love which existed between them.

The simple and true definition of love rests with a person's admiration of his fellow man's qualities while at the same time remaining aware of his own shortcomings. This humble position, the source of love, stood in contrast to Amalek's arrogance, preaching the greatness of some at the expense of others, a formula for distrust and hatred. Additionally, the role of the *tzaddik* is to sweeten the five existing types of judgments and to convert them to the five types of compassion. The five mystical channels of judgment are sweetened at their root through the intermediary of the upper *mazal*.

This act of appeasement of the divine decrees is performed each day during the five readings of the Megillah starting on the eleventh day of Adar. During these days in the month of Adar, the lives of Am Yisrael are guided by the heavenly attributes of kindness.[43]

The Megillah is read five times, "not less or more," to soften the five types of harsh judgments. Therefore, the Torah commands us to wipe out

42 *Midrash Tanchuma*, Deuteronomy 9

43 *Chesed, Gevurah, Tiferet, Netzach,* and *Hod* — are attributes of kindness through which God runs the world. When man prays and does good deeds, the Divine Light channels the *shefah* (abundance) through these *sefirot*, then to the *Sefirah* of *Yesod* before it is released to the last of the ten *sefirot, Malchut*, and then into our world. When man sins, he disturbs this structural order and empowers the *Sefirah* of *Gevurah* (judgment) to channel harsh judgment through these five *Sefirot* onto *Yesod*, then *Malchut*.

the memory of Amalek: "תמחה את זכר עמלק" – "erase the memory of Amalek." If we remove from עמלק, which equals 240, its זכר, memory, which is equal to 227, the resulting balance is 13, which is *ahavah*, love. So it is definitely possible in our time to continue fulfilling this commandment, just like all other commandments, by showering each other with love on one hand, and by avoiding conceit, the trait of Amalek. Since, according to the Arizal, love represents one of God's ineffable names, His name will become complete when Am Yisrael acts with love toward each other. As a result of total love between Am Yisrael, an encompassing love will spread among all the nations and all animal life, where the "wolf shall cohabit with the lamb."

The Torah relates that during the battle with Amalek, when Moses raised his hands, the Jews overpowered the enemy. The Sages ask: "Did the hands of Moses wage war to determine its outcome? Rather, they conclude, when the Jews lifted their eyes toward Heaven in a sign of submission, they were winning."[44] The truth is one need not lift his eyes to Heaven to submit his heart to God. Also, why do they need to look up to Moses to achieve this submission to Heaven? Moses, out of his exceptional humility, viewed every Jew as being greater than him. It is this very teaching which he tried to instill in the hearts of Am Yisrael. Each one should view his neighbor as better than himself in order to develop a strong love for that person. So when, in the midst of their battle, Am Yisrael lifted their eyes and looked up to see their neighbor, their love for each other grew stronger, and they overpowered the enemy.

The Sages explain that the *efod* worn by the High Priest atoned for the sin of slander, a derivative of conceit, the attribute of Amalek.[45] In order to win this battle against Amalek and its angel, the High Priest wore the *efod*, about which the verse says: "לפיו סביב מעשה אורג" – "its opening shall have a border all around."[46] The first letters of each word in this verse form the word סמול, Amalek's angel. Hence, אפוד was spelled fully in the verse to include the *vav* so that this garment, מעיל האפוד has the numerical value of 244, which equals the numerical value of עמלק

44 BT *Rosh Hashana* 29a

45 BT *Zevachim* 88b

46 Exodus 28:32

(240 plus 4 for the number of letters in the word) to atone for the sin of haughtiness, the source of *lashon hara*, evil speech. ■

RACHEL'S CHILDREN FIGHT AMALEK THROUGHOUT THE GENERATIONS

Throughout history, all pursuits and wars against Israel represent a logical follow-up to Amalek's first attack against the Jews – his war being an open defiance of God, and the Jews being the bearers of God's message.[47] When Amalek, the driving force of Evil, is wiped out, then, the final *tikkun* will be completed and God's Name will be crowned across the land, in accordance with Zechariah's prophecy: "Hashem will be the King over all the land; on that day Hashem will be One and His Name will be One."[48]

Appointing a king, wiping out the memory of Amalek and building the Beit Hamikdash were the first three commandments that Israel had to fulfill following their conquest of the Land of Canaan. If the Temple were to become the seat to the Divine Presence, and impress the Divine Glory upon all visitors, then Amalek who seeks to eliminate Godliness from the surface of the earth must first be eliminated. Although King Saul failed in his mission when he waged war against Amalek, still, he weakened the enemy to an extent which permitted God's Presence to dwell in the Temple, albeit with a restricted dimension. As long as evil overtly thrives, God's Name cannot wholly settle in the midst of mankind.

King Saul who fought Amalek, and Mordechai who brought down Haman, were both from the tribe of Benjamin who was not born yet when Jacob bowed before the wicked Esau. It seems there was dissatisfaction in heaven with Jacob over this action. It follows that only a descendant of Benjamin would confront Amalek, and only the tribe of Benjamin would merit hosting the Beit Hamikdash in its allotted portion of the Land of Israel.

47 R. Kotler, *Mishnat Rabbi Aaron*, III, Purim
48 Zechariah 14:9

In addition, Jewish tradition[49] insists that the final fall of Amalek will be at the hands of Rachel's children:[50] "The house of Jacob will be fire, the house of Joseph a flame, and the house of Esau for straw... There will be no survivor to the house of Esau." The fire (Joseph) will ignite and devour the straw (Esau). Elaborating on this point, the Midrash[51] explains that the man who stated "I (Joseph) fear God"[52] has earned the merit to avenge the divine glory from the one about whom it is written: "and he [Amalek] did not fear God."[53] The root to evil is the absence of God's fear. Following the redemption from Egypt and the splitting of the Red Sea, all nations heard and trembled except for Amalek. Hence, Joshua, the grandson of Joseph, was rightly chosen to lead the first war against Amalek when Israel was attacked. This might explain why, in Messianic Times, Mashiach ben Yosef will wage the first wars against the bearers of evil, preceding the advent of Mashiach ben David. King Saul failed in his mission and lost the crown because, in his justification to Samuel, he declared: "for I feared the people."[54] The anointed, or any Jew for that matter, must fear no one but God.

Although the Temple is no longer with us, Am Yisrael is still able to draw the Divine Presence within our midst. Thanks to Torah study, we can perpetuate the war against Amalek from generation to generation, weaken Evil and participate in the realization of the final *tikkun*. ■

49 Rashi, Genesis 31:1

50 Obadiah 1:18

51 *Midrash Rabbah*, Shemot 26:3

52 Genesis 42:18

53 Deuteronomy 25:18

54 I Samuel 15:24

Shabbat

Shabbat

*Our Sages explain that during the six days of Creation, the world was "restless" until the arrival of the Shabbat. Then the universe settled peacefully. During those six days of Creation, all the elements found themselves distanced from their Divine Source, because the process of Creation was accomplished through a series of contractions and expansions of the Divine Light, whereby each created world was of a higher spiritual state than the world below it, and so on until our final physical world. Hence, the created elements and planets ended up far from their Source. It was not until the seventh day that God permeated the newly created worlds with the holiness of the Shabbat. At that time, the created elements longed to connect with their Source. This process is referred to as "*aliyat ha'olamot,*" the elevation of the created worlds – a spiritual progress from down below to higher spheres until they could unite with the* Ein Sof, *blessed be His name. On the seventh day, all of creation longed to return to its Source.*

Spiritual Preparation Enhances Shabbat

During Israel's wandering in the Wilderness, God commanded that they build a Sanctuary for His Presence. He informed Moses that Betzalel has been designated to execute the artful work of building the holy Mishkan along with its vessels. At the same time, Israel is cautioned once again, about the observance of Shabbat. Clarifying this association, the Sages explain that the construction of the Sanctuary must not supersede the commandment to refrain from working on Shabbat: "Hashem spoke to Moses saying: 'See, I have called by the name Betzalel, the son of Uri, the son of Hur, of the tribe of Judah. I have filled him with a Godly spirit, with wisdom, insight, and knowledge and with every craft... However, you must observe My Shabbat, for it is a sign between Me and you for your generations, to know that I am Hashem, Who makes you holy…'"[1]

It seems that this requirement should have been conveyed earlier, in Terumah where all the details of building the Mishkan are stated.[2] The emphasis on the observance of Shabbat should have been made there to indicate that the manual tasks involved in constructing the Sanctuary must not take precedence over resting on Shabbat. So why is the commandment to observe Shabbat juxtaposed with the call to Betzalel? Also, the text suggests that the children of Israel will confer upon the Shabbat a lasting holiness. How could this be when we know that Shabbat was already sanctified at Creation?

The holy Zohar explains that the building of the Mishkan in the wilderness was a reflection of the creation of the world. God's pristine purpose for creating the universe was to reveal His Kingship to mankind, who would welcome Him as their King. When the nations of the world proclaim God as their Ruler and Creator, they "give Him an exceptional feeling of pride and satisfaction," as it were. As a result, God showers all His creatures with love, peace, and abundance. With the winding paths of history, generations erred and cut themselves off from God, and pushed the Divine Presence away from mankind. In order to rectify this damage, God commanded the Jewish People to build the Mishkan – a holy site for

1 Exodus 31:1–3
2 *Maor Vashemesh*, Ki Tissa

His dwelling among man. Just as Creation was accomplished with God's wisdom, insight, and knowledge, so was Betzalel inspired with wisdom, insight, and knowledge to achieve his noble mission.

This corroborates our Sages' teaching that Betzalel, who was filled with a Godly spirit, was aware of the correct combinations of the Torah characters by which the heaven and earth were created.[3] Just as God created the world with wisdom, insight and knowledge: "Hashem founded the earth with wisdom, He established the heavens with understanding; through His knowledge, the depths were cleaved...,"[4] He imbued Betzalel with the same attributes to build the Mishkan: "He filled him with Godly spirit, with wisdom, insight, and knowledge..."[5] Since God's intent in building the Mishkan was to dwell in the midst of mankind, He inspired Betzalel with the same mystical hidden combinations of divine names which enabled the creation of the world. In the course of performing his tasks, Betzalel was able to maintain the proper spiritual meditation (*kavanah*), conferring upon the Mishkan and its vessels the original objective of Creation. Through his *kavanah*, the Divine Presence would once more settle in our midst.

Granted, the concept of creating a physical object and of imbuing it with a spirituality powerful enough to draw upon it God's Presence is difficult to comprehend. Nonetheless, the Torah Jew whose intellect is refined and pure will not object to this supernatural singularity. The most striking proof is obtained from the observance of the Shabbat. On this day, explains the Zohar, every Jew receives a *neshama yeteirah*, a supplementary soul. It is through this *neshama* that everyone experiences the unique holiness of Shabbat and feels a special affinity with God.

It is noteworthy that the holiness of this extra *neshama* varies with the spiritual level of each individual. Some are granted a *neshama* from *Olam HaAsiyah*, the world of Completion, which is our cosmic system. Others receive it from a higher celestial sphere, *Olam HaYetzirah*, the world of Formation, or from *Olam HaBriah*, the world of Creation, or

---

3 Zohar Terumah 152
4 Proverbs 3:19-20
5 Exodus 35:31

from *Olam HaAtzilut*, the higher world of Emanation. It all depends on how much spiritual preparedness one invests in readying himself for the Shabbat. Some begin this process as late as Shabbat eve; others start as early as the first day of the week, where each physical activity is preceded by a *kavanah*. Hence, even today one is able to imprint his daily activities with spirituality.

God called upon Betzalel to build the Mishkan and its vessels. These articles would attract the Divine Presence because of Betzalel's spiritual wisdom, insight, and knowledge, which he instilled into the product of his artful hands. Anticipating man's skepticism on the feasibility of mingling holiness with a vessel made from gold, silver, or copper to such a degree as to pull down God's Presence from Heaven to earth, God pointed out the observance of the Shabbat as a clear proof of this lofty paradox. Hence, the call to Betzalel is adjoined with the observance of the Shabbat. Through the Shabbat, God makes us holy: "to know that I am Hashem, Who makes you holy." On account of the special Shabbat holiness, it is possible to invite a stronger divine revelation into our homes on Shabbat by infusing spiritual awareness into our daily activities on weekdays. Since intellectual capabilities vary widely from one group to another, it would be expected that some people will lack the faculty of applying a spiritual awareness to their physical occupation, which in turn would dim, for these people at least, the holiness of Shabbat. Consequently, the Torah states: "to make the Shabbat for their generations." This represents an invitation to the righteous of each generation to utilize their individual spiritual greatness to draw and spread upon all the holiness of Shabbat.

Our Sages explain that during the six days of Creation, the world was "restless" until the arrival of the Shabbat. Then the universe settled peacefully. During those six days of Creation, all the elements found themselves distanced from their divine Source, because the process of Creation was accomplished through a series of contractions and expansions of the Divine Light, whereby each created world was of a higher spiritual state than the world below it, and so on until our final physical world. Hence, the created elements and planets ended up far from their Source. It was not until the seventh day that God permeated the newly created worlds with the holiness of the Shabbat. At that time, the created elements longed to connect with their Source. This process is referred to as "*aliyat ha'olamot*," the elevation of the created worlds – a spiritual progress from down below to higher spheres until they could unite with the *Ein Sof*, blessed be His name. On the seventh day, all of creation longed to return to its Source.

As God rested on the seventh day, the holiness of Shabbat permeated the world and brought it serenity. We see that man is also able to draw holiness upon himself and his activities, and transform his physical body and surroundings into a recipient for the Divine Presence, just as Betzalel brought upon the material articles of the Mishkan the divine holiness. ■

Renewal of the Six Days of Creation

The Ohr Hachaim explains that the world was created to last only six days.[6] The text clearly states: "*ki sheshet yamim assah Hashem*" – "for God made six days." The text does not read: "*ki besheshet yamim assah Hashem*" – "for in six days God made the heavens and the earth." Continues the Ohr Hachaim, it is the observance of the ensuing Shabbat which re-energizes and renews Creation for another six days. Since the beginning of time, the holiness of Shabbat was always observed to reinvigorate the process of Creation. From Adam to Methuselah, from Noah to Abraham, all the way to our days, there never was a generational lapse when Shabbat was not observed.[7] Even if only one righteous person respects the holiness of Shabbat, the continuation of Creation is assured, otherwise the world will reverse to its pristine stage of astounding emptiness and darkness. In sum, the lifeline to Creation rests with our continuous Shabbat observance. Thus in the Ten Commandments, the Jewish People is urged: "Remember the Shabbat day to sanctify it. Six days shall you work and accomplish all your work; but the seventh day is Shabbat to Hashem, your God; you shall not do any work… For in six days Hashem made the heavens and the earth, the sea and all that is in them, and He rested on the seventh day. Therefore, Hashem blessed the Shabbat day and sanctified it."[8]

6 Genesis 2:3

7 R. Friedman, *Shvilei Pinchas*, Bereshit 5770

8 Exodus 20:8-12

In light of the above, on Shabbat, we add to the after-meal blessing: "Let there be neither distress nor grief on the day of our rest." It is a line which does not appear in the weekday blessing. However, since the following six days are regenerated by the Shabbat holiness, then all its blessings will automatically pervade the next six days of the week.[9] This idea concurs with the Zohar's teaching that all the heavenly blessings which descend upon the world originate from the blessings which flow to the world on Shabbat.[10]

Yet, we cannot help but underscore, albeit with humility and tremor, the following contradiction. If Creation derives its renewed energy from the previous Shabbat, how did the first six days come to exist without a preceding Shabbat? The Rav MeRimanov suggests that God's intention, as it were, to create the world was conceived at *mincha* time on the Shabbat preceding the first six days.[11] Although the concept of time did not yet exist, the holiness of Shabbat, being above the laws of nature, did exist. It is that divine intent that provided a sustaining lifeline to the first six days of Creation. The Talmud corroborates this proposition with a disclosure which God made to Moses when he received the Torah at Sinai: "In My treasures, I have a special gift which I wish to give Israel. It is Shabbat."[12] Clearly, we see that Shabbat surpasses the created world as it belonged to God's inner circle. Shabbat was not part of Creation because it already existed.

Moreover, the Zohar teaches that on a regular week day, the afternoon is the moment when the *dinim*, harsh judgments, descend upon the world.[13] It is not so on Shabbat. The midday hours are times of compassion. During *mincha* of Shabbat we call on God's mercy: "*Va'ani tefillati lecha Hashem et-ratzon*" – "as for me, may my prayer to You, Hashem, be at a time of favor. O God, in Your abundant kindness, respond to me with Your true deliverance."[14] Shabbat afternoon is *et-ratzon*, a time of favor, because that is the moment when God contemplated creating the

9 Bnei Yissachar, *Shabbatot* 7:13
10 Zohar, Yitro 88a
11 Quoted by the Rapshitz Rav, Chukkat
12 BT *Shabbat* 10b
13 Zohar, Terumah 156a
14 Psalms 69:14

world. So, when the first day came into being, it was preceded by the first evening: "And there was evening and there was morning, one day."[15] This is the very first Motzaei Shabbat which God conceived on Shabbat at *mincha et-ratzon*, a time of exceptional divine favorable disposition.

Now we can shed light on the Talmud's claim in the name of Rabbi Shimon bar Yochai: "Israel would immediately be redeemed when they will observe two consecutive Shabbats."[16] To which two days of Shabbat does the Talmud refer to? It is the spirit of the first Shabbat, which was above the concept of time, and which energized the first six days of Creation. It is also the second Shabbat which saw the completion of Creation and injected in it a perpetual force of renewal.

Likewise, the Talmud debates a case where one finds himself in the desert and is completely unaware of the day of the week.[17] How should he approach the observance of Shabbat? Rav Hunah holds that this individual should count six days and then rest on the seventh. Chiah bar Rav suggests that he should rather, observe one day as Shabbat, and count six days. Rav Hunah understands that Shabbat's role is to reinvigorate the previous six days. That explains his position to first count six days and rest on the seventh. While Chiah bar Rav seems to hold that the holiness of Shabbat inspires the upcoming six days. That is why one must first sanctify Shabbat, and then count six days. In reality, both Sages agree on the intrinsic significance of Shabbat.[18] It is above our concept of time, and that it regenerates the power of Creation.

Quoting the Zohar, the Baal HaTurim explains that the first Hebrew word in the Torah, **בראשית**, "In the Beginning [of God's creating the heavens and the earth],"[19] should be split into two words to appreciate its full significance: **ירא שבת** – the reverence of Shabbat, implying that Creation is perpetuated through the observance of Shabbat.[20] ■

15 Genesis 1:5

16 BT *Shabbat* 118b

17 Ibid., 69b

18 Author of *Avnei Nezer*, Neot HaDesheh, I. 4,

19 Genesis 1:1

20 *Tikkun* 9 24b

SHABBAT IS THE PURPOSE OF CREATION

Rabbi Chaim Vital reveals that God is the epitome of goodness whose natural propensity is to bestow unrestrained kindness. It is to this effect that God created the universe to spoil, as it were, His creatures with infinite benevolence. As a result, mankind will recognize and faithfully worship their Creator.

Yet, we are all witness to a world mostly marked by cruelties rather than by thoughtfulness.[21] Like a relentless gale, yesterday's calamities are overshadowed by today's misfortunes. Where then, do we find the promised flow of abundance, of tranquility and joyfulness?

Addressing this issue, the *Maor Vashemesh* explains that God's bequests are commensurate with His perfection.[22] As the latter is infinite so will His gifts be boundless. However, in our finite world, there exists an imbalance between the unlimited powers of the Giver and the physical restrictions of the recipient. It is only in the World to Come, where the soul is no longer restrained by the physical boundaries of the body, that man can receive the endless divine flow of goodness.

Likewise, the *Mesilat Yesharim* adds that this world is but a preparatory stage to earning entry to the world of eternal bliss where God's kindness is dispensed without limitation.[23] Thanks to man's good deeds and the fulfillment of the Torah commandments, he will merit dwelling close to God and discovering the mysteries of Creation. This is the idea of: "*az tit'anag al Hashem,* then you will have delight in Hashem."[24] In its proximity to the Divine Light, the soul will have access to a boundless knowledge of Godliness.

Since the World to Come constitutes the true purpose of our journey through life, it leads that Shabbat equally represents the objective of Creation, because on this day, a Jew experiences a taste of *Olam Habbah*

21 R. Berzovsky , *Netivot Shalom*, Shabbat 4
22 Noach
23 Chapter 1
24 Isaiah 58:13

through the holiness of Shabbat. On this day, the observant Jew detaches himself from all forms of material pursuits, and enjoys a unique spiritual closeness to God. So, on Shabbat, we invoke the prophet's words over the wine cup: "*az tit'anag al Hashem*" – "then you will have delight in Hashem." Notwithstanding the prevalent darkness and life's anxieties, the holiness of Shabbat sheds a ray of purpose transcending the daily challenges.

The sanctification of the seventh day is noted in Genesis at the conclusion of the six days of Creation: "Thus the heaven and the earth were finished, and their entire array… God blessed the seventh day and sanctified it…"[25] This line should rather figure in Leviticus 23, with the list of holidays which the Jewish People observe throughout the year. But it is mentioned here because the sanctity of Shabbat is an integral part of Creation. In the same way that the World to Come represents Creation's objective, so does Shabbat constitute the purpose of Creation. It is as if a spectacular palace is built without any lighting. The palace is practically useless. So would seem the six days of Creation without Shabbat. *Shabbat Kodesh* is the radiating light into a Jew's material and spiritual life. ■

SHABBAT'S SANCTITY IMPACTS THE HOLIDAYS

"Hashem spoke to Moses saying: Speak to the Children of Israel and say to them: Hashem's appointed festivals that you are to designate as holy convocations…"[26] It is clear that the text's wording suggests that God granted Israel the authority to designate the holidays' timing. As only the Rabbinical Court proclaims the beginning of the New Moon, then the Hebrew calendar, to include the holidays, is closely dependant on the timing of the first of the month. It follows that Yom Kippur will fall ten days after the start of Tishrei, and Sukkot will be on the fifteenth. This incredible concept, where Israel is granted control over time, highlights the unique relationship between God and Am Yisrael.

However, Shabbat's holiness was proclaimed by God at the conclusion of the six days of Creation. This fact dictates that Creation is di-

25 Genesis 2:1

26 Leviticus 23:4 – *tikre'u otam,* rather, read as *tikre'u atem*

vinely designed for a holy purpose, and that it is not a casual event. Man's presence in the world along with his ideas must mirror this objective.

Moreover, all the Jewish holidays draw their sanctity from Shabbat's holiness.[27] As God sealed Creation with the holiness of the seventh day, He imbued the remaining holidays with the potential of gaining their individual sanctity from Shabbat. Since the holiness of Shabbat is part of Creation, it enables the other holidays to feed off its sanctity. Consequently, the Mechilta reveals that God promised Israel that they will merit experiencing the holiness of Pesach, Atzeret and Sukkot if they observe Shabbat.[28] It is because these three holidays derive their sanctity from Shabbat's holiness.

This also explains why the Shabbat preceding Pesach is called Shabbat HaGadol. In order to experience the holiness of Pesach, the newly formed nation of Israel needed a spiritual boost from the first Shabbat which saw the Jews accepting the first set of divine commandments.

As God proclaims Shabbat an everlasting covenant between Him and Israel, it follows that no other nation is honored with Shabbat's holiness. Israel earned this eternal privilege through their suffering under Egyptian slavery which purified their soul: "Between Me and the Children of Israel it is a sign forever."[29]

The Midrash adds in the name of Rabbi Shimon bar Yochai that Shabbat remarked that every day of the week is paired with its mate, except for itself.[30] Sunday is followed by Monday; Tuesday is coupled with Wednesday, and Thursday with Friday. God responded that Israel shall be Shabbat's soul mate. In fact, no other day of the week could have made such a claim save for Shabbat. As God's glory is revealed to the world each day, through the myriad of elements created on that day, then, His Kingship is acknowledged across the world. The created elements represent the soul mate to that specific day. However, on Shabbat, nothing was created to reveal God's glory. To this objective, God assigned the holy people to the

27 R. Sherer *Ohr Gedaliahu*, Shabbat HaGadol
28 Beshalach 16
29 Exodus 31:17
30 *Bereshit Rabbah* 11:9

sanctified day. Israel will praise Him and spread His greatness: "A psalm, a song for the Shabbat day. It is good to thank Hashem and to sing praise to Your Name, O Exalted One."[31] Thus God expresses, as it were, His gratitude to and pride of Am Yisrael: "*Am zu yatzarti li tehillati yesaperu*" – "this people which I fashioned for Myself that they might declare My praise."[32]

"*Bereshit*," in the beginning, is the first word in Genesis which the Sages read as *bishvil reshit*, on account of the beginning – that is, Israel – God created the heavens and the earth. In other words, God proceeded with His plan to create the universe because of Israel who would worship and praise Him. Likewise, Shabbat was not part of Creation, as it already existed. The Talmud corroborates this suggestion with a disclosure which God made to Moses when he received the Torah at Sinai: "In My treasures, I have a special gift which I wish to give Israel. It is Shabbat."[33] Clearly, we see that Shabbat surpasses the created world as it already existed. Shabbat and Israel form a perfect match as they both share in common God's original intention. Shabbat, from the Hebrew word *shav*, equally invokes the idea of *teshuvah*, inviting a Jew to find spiritual harmony by returning to his Source. ■

A Taste of Olam Habbah

"By the seventh day God completed His work which He had done, and He abstained on the seventh day from all His work which He had done."[34] Shabbat implies the perfection of Creation.[35] It invokes the successful crowning moments of a process. It defines the serenity which descended upon a new world. It is like a king who built a magnificent palace which lacked nothing except a bride. The Shabbat brings to the material world the spirituality it lacked. The restfulness of Shabbat has nothing to do with idleness, rather; it is an expression of our spiritual pursuit and a detachment from the physical activities of the week. Shabbat affirms that

31 Psalms 92:1
32 Isaiah 43:21
33 BT *Shabbat* 10b
34 Genesis 2:2
35 R. Eliyahu Dessler, *Michtav Me'Eliyahu* II,

Creation has a spiritual purpose. Most importantly, it states that there is no inconsistency between the physical world and the spiritual life. Thanks to Shabbat, one is able to infuse holiness into all his material activities.

Surely, God did not exert Himself in any way to refrain from work, so what defines His physical exertion? It is an expression of His will by which He creates the concealment of His Presence enabling man to utilize his free choice and discover Godliness. The physical world represents a veiled curtain, our role is to remove the obscure veils and find God's radiance. Likewise, God's abstention from work translates into a withdrawal of the Divine Presence as an act of kindness toward man to find God through his own efforts. Shabbat's holiness constitutes the perfect medium by which to achieve this spiritual objective.

This being the case why is Am Yisrael commanded to honor Shabbat with lit candles, wine, delicious meals and beautiful clothes? Where is the spiritual drive in these culinary manifestations? It is man's inclination to express his joy with good drinks and foods and regal clothing. He will automatically come to honor the Shabbat through these delights. The challenge is to focus on the holiness of Shabbat and not on one's palate. In a chain-like fashion, man will equally concentrate on the path which will lead him to *Olam Habbah*. How? By assigning a secondary status to all worldly needs and desires, and view those purely as a vehicle to gaining access to *Olam Habbah*. Through the delights of Shabbat, one can easily find and follow the thread leading to the eternal happiness of *Olam Habbah*.

The first historical occurrence when time was blessed is when God blessed the seventh day. This in itself creates a paradox. Blessing implies an unrestricted spread of abundance while time indicates a limitation. How could the seventh day which is restrained time become the recipient of unrestrained blessings? On account of its holiness, Shabbat is beyond the boundaries of time. This is the reason it is blessed. Likewise, in *Olam Habbah*, the concept of limitation and time are unknown; instead, it is identified with eternity. Am Yisrael earns access to *Olam Habbah* thanks to Shabbat observance, as one carries into his weekly activities the holiness of Shabbat. The Midrash[36] relays that during the Giving of the Torah, God

36 *Otiyot De Rabbi Akiva*, quoted in *Michtav Me'Eliyahu* II, chap. 1

addressed Am Yisrael: "My children, it is My wish to grant you a precious gift if you guard My Torah." "What is the gift?" They asked. "It is *Olam Habbah*." He replied. "Master of the Universe! Show us an example of *Olam Habbah*." They inquired. God answered: "It is Shabbat, it represents one sixtieth of *Olam Habbah*." ■

THE PRECIOUS GIFT OF THE NESHAMA YETEIRAH

The Talmud[37] reveals that at the onset of Shabbat, every Jew receives from heaven a *neshama yeteirah*, which is taken back the following night at the conclusion of Shabbat.

What is the essence of the *neshama yeteirah*? Rashi points at the unique Shabbat feeling of peace, relaxation and joyfulness.[38] He equally associates it with the ease with which one consumes multiple course meals without physical impediment. It enables a person to delight in the Shabbat and to connect with God.

What is the purpose of the *neshama yeteirah*? According to our Sages, it is our observance and sanctification of Shabbat which guarantees Creation's continuation.[39] The holiness of Shabbat perpetually injects renewed energy into God's work. As it were, on this day, God provides us with a complimentary soul as a tool to fulfill our role as partner with Him in maintaining the world's continuity. In sum, the lifeline to Creation rests with our continuous Shabbat observance. Since this heavy responsibility depends upon the commitment of the Jewish People, God granted every individual the *neshama yeteirah* as a helping device to acquit himself of this stupefying duty. In alluding to this mystical event, King Solomon writes:[40] "For the living know that they will die, but the dead know nothing at all." On Shabbat, the righteous who make the most of their *neshama yeteirah* experience the meaning of life, knowing that they will die, that is, the *neshama yeteirah* will depart from them at the ending of Shabbat. As the

37 BT *Beitzah* 16a
38 Ibid.
39 Genesis 2:3
40 Ecclesiastes 9:5

neshama leaves its imprint for the rest of the week, they are referred to as "the living." On the other hand, those who misuse the potential of their *neshama yeteirah* are referred to as "dead," even when they are alive. With this information in hand, the recipient must not squander the holiness of Shabbat in the pursuit of frivolous activities. Rather, he should optimize every moment of that day with prayer and Torah study.[41] In maximizing the sanctity of Shabbat, the individual will successfully carry the holiness he experienced into his weekly occupations.[42]

In line with the above, it becomes clearer why God refers to Shabbat as "a precious gift which I wish to give Israel.[43] Is all the Torah not precious? In order to realize a *tikkun* in the upper worlds, every commandment necessitates an active participation or a physical act. It is the individual's performance of the commandment which triggers in heaven the specific spiritual reparation to man's sins. It is not so with Shabbat. On this day, the *tikkun* is initiated by God, while the Jewish individual simply refrains from the thirty-nine categories of prohibited activities. The Zohar refers to this mystical concept as "*it'aruta dil'eilah*," – "an awakening from above" – the *tikkun* is initiated by God. It ennobles Shabbat with the special title of "a precious gift."

Additionally, the Sages state that whoever sanctifies Shabbat – through blessing over the wine – is viewed as if he joined hands with God in creating the world.[44] It is because a Jew justifies Creation's renewal by observing Shabbat. Now this person is partner with God's work.

The conclusion of Shabbat is celebrated with a *seudah* known as "King David's meal." God informed King David that his death would take place on Shabbat. However, King David did not know which Shabbat it would be. So he spent the entire Shabbat immersed in Torah study and prayers. He gave thanks for his life with celebration at the conclusion of each Shabbat. Likewise, we also commemorate Creation's renewal at the end of Shabbat with a special meal.

41 *Zichron Tov*, the Chozeh MiLublin in the name of the Baal Shem Tov
42 R. Friedman, *Shvilei Pinchas*, Ki Tissa 5767
43 BT *Shabbat* 10b
44 Ibid., 119b

It is clear that, with the observance of Shabbat, the Jewish People carries a laudable and heavy responsibility. Shabbat is not just a day of rest; it impacts the well-being of the created worlds and the divine blessings they receive. ■

Rosh Chodesh

Rosh Chodesh

In Egypt, God showered Am Yisrael with kindness by taking the initiative to deliver them, notwithstanding their decadence. Just as the moon goes through a renewal process, God was convinced that the Jewish People would come out of its spiritual darkness and merit to witness the Sinai Revelation. Like the moon, Israel's power for renewal represents their enduring characteristic. This is the built-in message in the commandment to utilize the lunar cycle. God expects Israel to constantly renew their religious devotion. Notwithstanding the spitefulness or the immorality of the host cultures, it is God's desire that the Jew will always recognize the ray of light enabling him to overcome the darkness of hostile surroundings.

The Rule of God over the Universe

The Hebrew calendar is closely dependant on the first of the month. In His intricate relationship with the Jewish People, God granted Israel control over time: "Speak to the Children of Israel and say to them: Hashem's appointed festivals that you are to designate as holy convocations..."[1] God empowered the Rabbinical Court to proclaim the beginning of the New Moon. This concept clearly demonstrates that Israel's destiny is above the laws of nature and time.

"This month shall be for you the beginning of months..."[2] The Jewish calendar is based on the lunar months and not on the solar months. The sun has no visible monthly cycle, but the moon has a visible renewable cycle. The Hebrew word for "month" – "*chodesh*" also means "new." It is therefore evident that the Torah is teaching us to adopt the lunar cycle, since the sun does not possess a visible renewable cycle.[3]

However, God commanded that the celebration of Pesach and Sukkot always take place in the spring and in the fall respectively. The holidays are referred to as the "Festival of Spring" and the "Festival of Harvest Time." Had we undertaken to base our calendar solely on the lunar months, these two holidays would sometimes fall in the summer and other times in the middle of the winter. To avoid this situation, we adopted a calendar based on both the lunar and solar cycles. The yearly solar cycle is completed every 365 days and 6 hours. The yearly lunar cycle requires 12 months, each of which is comprised of 29 days 12 hours and 793 portions of the hour (793/1,080 — Chazal divided the hour into 1,080 portions). When multiplied by 12, the lunar year comes out to be 354 days 8 hours and 876 hourly portions. Thus the solar year exceeds the lunar year by 10 days 21 hours and 204 hourly portions. These additional ten days cannot be ignored — over a period of time, they add up to cause a discrepancy between the lunar year and the solar year which determines the four seasons. In order to balance these cycles, our Sages decided to accumulate the ten extra days in three years into one additional month

1 Leviticus 23:4 – *tikre'u otam*, rather, read as *tikre'u atem*
2 Exodus 12:2
3 *Torah Temimah*, Exodus 12:2

and establish a leap year. With this approach, we also meet the Torah requirement to count full months for the year and not a month plus a few days.[4] The Talmud derives this instruction from the directive given to Moshe: "This month shall be for you the beginning of the months, it shall be for you the first of the months of the year."[5] Only full months will make up the year and not months and extra days.

The four letter name of Hashem, *yud keh vav keh*, is vowelized depending on the *Sefirah* it invokes.[6] It associates *Keter* with *kamatz*, *Chochmah* with *patach*, *Binah* with *tzerei*, *Chessed* with *segol*, *Gevurah* with *shevah*, *Tiferet* with *cholam*, *Netzach* with *hirik*, *Hod* with *kubutz*, *Yesod* with *shuruk*, and *Malchut* is quiet without punctuation. The combination of Hashem's Name with the different vowels adds to 1,080. This corresponds to the 1,080 portions of each hour and signals that the maintenance of Creation takes place every moment through God's Name. In the *Yotzer* section of the Morning Prayer, we uphold this principle by declaring: "Who, in His goodness, renews everyday and constantly the work of Creation."[7] Creation is perpetuated thanks to the flow of God's *shefa*, radiating light of energy into the world.

Moreover, because Pesach must be celebrated in the spring, and since the month of Adar precedes the springtime, we add the thirteenth month after Adar and not to any other month. At that time, we are in a good position to evaluate the immediacy of the spring or its possible delay and so determine whether a leap year is needed. This is known as "*ibbur hashanah*." Additional consideration is taken into account when proclaiming a leap year. Since all of Am Yisrael needed to go to Jerusalem on Pesach to worship God at the Beit HaMikdash, the roads and bridges that were washed away by the heavy winter rains had to be repaired to remove any danger to the travelers. So the decision to make that year a leap year may have been based on a specific material need.

With regard to the moon, at the end of each month, when it lines up with the sun in the west, it becomes hidden for a day or two. Sub

---

4 BT *Megillah* 5a

5 Exodus 12:2

6 See p. 96 for additional comments about the ten *Sefirot*

7 *Likutim of Rav Issachar Dov Rubin zt"l*, *Nefesh HaChaim* 1:2

sequently, when the moon is visible again, it indicates the start of the new month for which we begin to count twenty-nine days. If the moon reappears on the eve of the thirtieth day, the new month begins on the thirtieth day, thus establishing the previous month as a *chodesh chaser*, a shorter month, because it had only twenty-nine days. When the moon reappears on the eve of the thirty-first day, the new month begins on the following day, making the previous month a *chodesh malei*, a full month of thirty days as opposed to twenty-nine days. This is what is referred to as *ibbur hachodesh.*

In his teachings, Rabbah bar Shmuel indicates that the *ibbur hachodesh*, unlike *ibbur hashanah*, must not be established on account of a particular need.[8] When the moon reappears, the new month is announced, without delay and without any other considerations, such as the desire to see Yom Kippur fall on a specific day of the week. Based on a specific need, the Beit Din may declare a regular year a leap year, but it may not proclaim a short month a full month.

The renewal of the moon is God's testimony to His rule over the universe. Hence, we stand to acknowledge His glory by reciting *Kiddush Levanah*, the blessing over the renewal of the moon, each month. Moreover, the concept of renewal represents an incentive to renew our bond with God through *teshuvah.*

Our Sages liken our world to a hallway, while the World to Come is likened to a spectacular palace. The idea is that it is through the hallway that one can enter the palace. It seems paradoxical that one is expected to gain access to *Olam Habbah* through the intermediary of a world filled with physical temptations which negate the concepts of holiness, sanctity and spirituality. Moreover, the Sages suggest that God created the world in order to dwell amongst mankind. This too presents a contradiction. How could His Glory find a holy site in the midst of unrestrained material desires and pursuits? In reality, one can acquire Godliness in every aspect of the physical world.

Thanks to the attribute of love which God implanted in one's heart, every Jew can find God through his possessions as well as nature's elements.

8 BT *Rosh Hashana* 20a

Even when a person is immersed in a sinful life, he is able to find God and return to Him when he contemplates his immoral behavior. Indeed, life's objective is to discover God no matter how concealed He seems to us. Just as we know with certainty that the moon will reappear following its temporary concealment, we should equally remain convinced of God's presence in all of life's circumstances. ■

THE HOPE OF THE NEW MOON

The Tur explains that the three holidays correspond to the three Patriarchs.[9] Pesach invokes Abraham's attribute of kindness, Shavuot recalls Isaac's fear of God, and Sukkot evokes Jacob's dedication to the truth, a balanced line between compassion and justice. As to the twelve *Rashei Chodashim*, beginning of the months of the year, they correspond to the attributes of the twelve tribes of Israel: "I will remember for them the covenant of the ancients."[10] In the same manner that a *brit*, a covenant, with the forefathers is present, there is also a *brit*, an eternal bond, between God and the tribes.[11] Confirming this everlasting relationship, the Talmud states that, regardless of the lengthy persecutions and displacements, no tribe of Israel shall ever disappear.[12]

Therefore, adds the Tur, Rosh Chodesh should equally be celebrated as a holiday in the same manner that we celebrate Pesach, Shavuot and Sukkot. During the days of the Temple, the Jewish People traveled to Jerusalem three times a year to rejoice in the presence of the Priests and the Levites. The reason the beginning of the month is not celebrated is on account of the Golden Calf sin. Since that infamous day, the *shefa*, the Divine Light unique to Rosh Chodesh, ceased to descend upon the world. Each holiday experiences a flow of divine blessings unique to that holiday. It is connected to the specific approach of worship pursued by each Patriarch. However, in Messianic Times, this restraint will be resolved and the twelve *Rashei Chodashim* will be celebrated: "It shall be

9 Orach Chaim 417
10 Leviticus 26:45
11 R. Sherer *Ohr Gedaliahu*, Rosh Chodesh Nissan
12 BT *Bava Batrah* 115b

that at every New Moon and on every Shabbat all mankind will come to prostrate themselves before Me, says Hashem."[13] The present concealment shall be unveiled and people shall show up in Jerusalem at the New Moon, because it will be celebrated as a *yom tov.*

Then the *shefa* which shall descend upon the world on Rosh Chodesh will be that of spiritual renewal. It is the idea forwarded by King David: "Hashem said to me, 'You are My son, I have begotten you this day.'"[14] For if man could feel that he was created today, he would see God's greatness in every aspect of life. The old habit of being around has interfered with this reality. Nonetheless, Rosh Chodesh is an opportunity to experience a renewed attachment with God.

Thus King David has an affinity with the New Moon. He daily felt the renewal of life with such intensity that he sang to God and composed many psalms praising the Creator. It is in this spirit that the episode with Bathsheba happened upon him so that the Jewish People would learn from him the power of *teshuvah.* Repentance is the highest expression of renewal as an individual starts a new beginning.

Generally, it is acceptable to evaluate the present based on future developments. When he waged war against the four kings, Abraham pursued them until the land of Dan and relented.[15] Abraham, the prophet, foresaw the idols which later in history the tribe of Dan would erect in that region and would lose the ardor to finish off the enemy. It seems that the evil that Abraham's progeny were to do in the future left an imprint on Abraham's present choice. Likewise, in the future, the unique *shefa* of Rosh Chodesh would descend upon the earth. This explains the reading of the incomplete *Hallel* on Rosh Chodesh although it is not a holiday. As Rosh Chodesh will become a *yom tov* at a future time, the *Hallel,* which is read only on *yom tov,* is recited at the present time.

While the calendar year begins in the month of Tishrei, the religious year begins in the month of Nissan. This is springtime, and Nissan

---

13 Isaiah 66:23

14 Psalms 2:7

15 BT *Sanhedrin* 36a

is identified with spiritual renewal. The Mishkan built by Betzalel and Moses in the Wilderness was inaugurated by the twelve tribe leaders during the first twelve days of Nissan. The first month of the year carries in full force the spirit of renewal. This is the reason Israel is compared to the moon which renews itself at a regular and visible cycle. Since the moon's brightness is dependent on the light it receives from the sun, so is Israel's existence solely dependent on God.

The Talmud relates the observation made by Rabbi Yochanan Ben Zakai when, soon after the destruction of Jerusalem, he ran into a young impoverished girl who came from a once prosperous family.[16] "Happy is your lot Israel; no nation can subdue you when you fulfill God's wish. But when you disobey Him, you fall into the hands of the basest rulers." Asks the Maharal: "Should Israel be thrilled when they are subjugated by a low nation?"[17] He then proceeds to explain that whether in greatness or exile, Israel is always under the direct stewardship of God. Like the moon which receives its brightness from the sun, Israel's destiny is devised by God. Being under the constant guidance of God is indeed reason to feel well placed pride. Similarly, the Land of Israel is too under God's direct supervision: "A land that Hashem, your God, seeks out; the eyes of Hashem, your God, are always upon it, from the beginning of the year to year's end."[18]

The holiness of the Land of Israel is so high that it is counterbalanced by a greater concentration of the *klipot*, the forces of destructions. The latter's dwelling places are within the hills and desolate areas of Israel. So, whenever a new construction project is initiated in the Land of Israel, these *klipot* are disturbed and pushed away from their inhabitation.[19] Then, they attach themselves to the leadership of surrounding nations, and turn into vocal opposition to Israel's settlements and growth. In order to deflect the nation's hostility and to weaken the raging *klipot*, the Sages urge that we intellectually attach ourselves to God and focus on holiness.[20] Only our clinging to God will silence the *klipot* and their carriers.

16 BT *Ketubot* 66b

17 Maharal, *Netzach Yisrael* 14

18 Deuteronomy 11:12

19 R. Menachem Nachum of Chernobyl, *Meor Einayim*, Ki Teitzei, *Netivot Shalom*, Shelach

20 Ibid., the supporting argument to this interpretation is in Ki Teitzei, Deut., 22:8

Likewise, the Talmud explains that General Naaman who was miraculously cured from leprosy by the prophet, abandoned idol worship and adopted the Noahide Laws, while Nebuzerradan, the Babylonian general who destroyed Jerusalem and murdered tens of thousands of its inhabitants became a *ger tzedek*, righteous convert.[21] In the midst of the unequaled destruction which he led, Nebuzerradan observed Israel's greatness and concluded it was only right to become one of them. Notwithstanding their devastation, Nebuzerradan realized that Israel's downfall was willed by God. On account of the unparalleled relationship with God, Israel's tragedy and splendor are testimonies to their greatness.

The nations of the world are likened to the sun because their own destiny lies with the laws of nature. It is not so with Israel who are compared to the moon. Just as the moon receives its light from the sun, so do Israel receive their *hanhaga*, their national or individual direction, from God. Their possessions are the result of God's kindness, not of their individual achievements. In the midst of their downfall, their prominence is visible.

Like the new moon, Rosh Chodesh holds a potential for renewed spiritual vigor for every Jew. It is a propitious time for introspection and rapprochement with God. ■

Israel's Power for Renewal

Shortly before the Israelites were to be freed from the Egyptian bondage, God informed Moses that, starting in the month of Nissan, Israel will adopt a lunar calendar: "This month shall be for you the beginning of the months, it shall be for you the first of the months of the year."[22] It is through this commandment that the precise timing of the Jewish holidays is determined. The Beit Din, who held its judicial sessions inside the Beit HaMikdash, would proclaim the sanctity of Rosh Chodesh, based on the testimony delivered by two witnesses who had observed a new moon. Rashi suggests that the Torah should have begun with this verse

21 Talmud *Gittin* 57b
22 Exodus 12:1

as it represents the first commandment given to the Jews as a nation.[23] It is noteworthy that until this time in history, all nations based their calendar year on the solar cycle. Following the Exodus from Egypt, the Jewish People adopted the lunar calendar while the Gentiles continued with the solar calendar. We would like to explore the significance of this commandment and further understand it.[24] Also, why was it delivered in Egypt proper and not at Sinai?

Toward the end of each lunar month, the moon's brightness fades away until it disappears, when it aligns itself behind the sun. While a period of darkness settles in, we remain aware that it is only temporary. Within a few days and without doubt, the moon will reappear in its full splendor. This infallible characteristic of the moon equally identifies the destiny of the Jewish People which has experienced numerous episodes of darkness and tragedies, convinced that these disturbing cycles are momentary.

Like the moon, Am Yisrael is convinced of upcoming brighter days and looks with a seasoned eye at the scorn by other nations. This commandment is thus addressed first, as it underscores Israel's faith in God. Notwithstanding all their turbulent history and suffering, in time Israel will experience a renewal and be a light unto the nations. This message is paramount to Jewish belief. Faith in God represents a fundamental tenet of Judaism. Israel's pain is not accidental. Its long years of suffering and national humility are the results of God's *hashgacha pratit,* divine involvement in small and large events. Thus Israel's greatness is manifest in its fall as much as it is in its rise. In the midst of their darkness, the Jews are focused on the upcoming ray of light which will shine, as surely as the moon's surface will lighten up again. Israel's confidence in God remains unaltered in their darkest moments as much as during their glory.

During the Haggadah reading, we evoke the slaying of the firstborn in the land of Egypt: "I [God] will pass through the land of Egypt; I, and no angel." It is evident that God Himself brought the tenth plague. He did not entrust this mission to an angel. This language leads us to deduct

23 Genesis 1:1

24 R. Berzovsky, *Netivot Shalom,* Bo

that the other plagues were dispatched at the hands of other emissaries such as angels. Why would God insist on delivering Himself the last and most fearsome plague? After spending two hundred and ten years in the heart of an immoral society, the Jews were forcibly influenced to adopt the corrupt mores of their hosts. They had no merits in their own rights to deserve redemption. However, God alone could penetrate into Israel's innermost essence and realize the potential for their spiritual greatness. This anticipation justified their redemption. An angel is not able to look beyond; he could not ignore their current failings. As he would not identify their merits, he would not act to save them.

In Egypt, God showered Am Yisrael with kindness by taking the initiative to deliver them, notwithstanding their decadence. Again, just as the moon goes through a renewal process, God was convinced that the Jewish People would come out of its spiritual darkness and merit to witness the Sinai Revelation. Like the moon, Israel's power for renewal represents their enduring characteristic. This is the built-in message in the commandment to utilize the lunar cycle. God expects Israel to constantly renew their religious devotion. Notwithstanding the spitefulness or the immorality of the host cultures, it is God's desire that the Jew will always recognize the ray of light enabling him to overcome the darkness of hostile surroundings.

We know for a fact that the renewal of the moon starts at the darkest point of the month. Like the night's slow progression, the full moon gradually flows to its full splendor. Similarly, Israel's redemption is approaching slowly but surely. ■

Afterword

It is said about a prince of a Kingdom who because of some objectionable behavior was banished by the King's court to an island. The people who lived in the island were reputed for their roughness and unscrupulous ways. Worried about the harmful influence on his son, the King brought him back to the royal court for short visits at regular intervals. He reasoned that with these visitations, the prince would continue to remember and maintain royal proprieties. Similarly, while in exile, the Jewish People is constantly recalled to be near God through the celebration of Shabbat and the Jewish holidays. Thanks to the depth of their spiritual message, the Jewish People will remain faithful to the laws of the Torah and continue to be a light unto the nations.

The Mishna teaches that anyone whose good deeds exceed his wisdom, then his wisdom will endure; but anyone whose wisdom exceeds his good deeds, his wisdom will not endure.[1] Every creation which God created in the world is contained within its protective boundaries.[2] For example, human organs are protected by the flesh and skin, and the eyes by the eyelids. If they outgrow the physical boundaries of the body they will be exposed to fatal dangers. The same is true for the animal and plant worlds. The ocean waves equally recognize their line of demarcation. Similarly, the physical containment of man's wisdom is his deeds. If the wisdom exceeds one's deeds, then all the wisdom will be exposed to falsehood and destructive ideas. Without its natural protection, his wisdom will not endure. More than man's wisdom, his actions are the true

1 *Avot* 3:12
2 R. Yisrael Mi'Rudgin

testimony to who he is. Therefore, the meticulous observance of Shabbat and Jewish holidays defines his love of God more than his knowledge does. The value of his deeds far outweighs his theoretical awareness. It is so because the objective of man's relationship with God is to cling to the Creator. This is the laudable Torah concept of *dvekut b'Hashem*. The ultimate perfection is achieved only if one becomes attached to God intellectually, but also through his actions. Since the Torah is comprised of 613 commandments, it offers 613 paths of clinging to God.[3] Any activities which compromise this goal must be abandoned as they erect a barrier between us and God. The observance of Shabbat and the holidays brings us closer to God. This is what King David vividly aspired to: "But as for me, God's nearness is my good."[4]

In the Talmud, Rabbi Eliezer states that Israel's redemption is assured only if they repent; otherwise there will be no redemption.[5] Disputing this suggestion, Rabbi Yehoshua rhetorically asks: "and if they do not repent, does it mean that they will not be redeemed?" Rather, he adds, "if the children of Israel do not repent, God will bring about a cruel leader whose decrees will be as harsh as Haman's and they will be forced to turn to Hashem and repent." Essentially, redemption will occur either through compassion – a smooth transition in world's events, or through frightful decrees, such as world wars, worrisome threats and condemnations. Moreover, Rabbi Shimon bar Yochai teaches that in the merit of Torah study and observance, one will be saved from the nations' sword.[6] Israel's redemption need not come through tumultuous world events and anxiety. It could proceed in a background of complete divine compassion. Eventually, our commitment to God's appointed holidays and Shabbat will define the road map to redemption.

When Rav Hunah's financial situation took a sudden downturn for the worse, the Talmud Sages of Babylon stopped by to comfort him.[7] Rav Hunah's four hundred barrels of exclusive wine unexpectedly turned sour and became vinegar. During the visitation, they subtly implied that

---

3 Zohar, Vayishlach
4 Psalms 73:28
5 BT *Sanhedrin* 97b
6 *Tana Debei Eliyahu*, 16:2
7 BT *Brachot* 5b

it is a good opportunity for some soul searching, for they concluded, all heavenly retributions represent a Divine response to man's flawed conduct.

The righteous Rav Hunah was understandably shaken by the Sages' allusion. "Are you suspecting a sinful behavior on my part," he incredulously asked?

"Would you suggest that God's justice is unfair?" they retorted.

"I cannot think of any wrongdoing on my part, but if you are aware of anything please tell me," Rav Hunah added.

Then, the Sages proceeded to explain what they heard about Rav Hunah withholding some payments in the form of vineyard crop to his farm tenant.

"You know he is a thief who stole my entire harvest!" claimed Rav Hunah.

The Sages remarked that they are fully aware of this situation, still it does not justify withholding the worker's payments.

Immediately, Rav Hunah answered: "*Kabbelnah alai*, I acknowledge my error and I am willing to rectify it. I will pay back what I owe."

The Talmud goes on to say that on that same night, the price of vinegar in the Middle East surged to the original value of wine. In other words, in a miraculous way, Rav Hunah regained his fortune through a favorable Divine intervention.

"*Kabbelnah alai*," was the magic word. When an individual is ready to acknowledge his mistakes and to repent, he unleashes heavenly forces able to shake the entire world on his behalf. Similarly, the tumultuous times the Jewish People is living through, along with the unrelenting threats and condemnations by surrounding nations necessitate that we all lift our hearts to God and cry out: "*Ribbono shel Olam! Kabbelnah alai!*" This represents the surest way we can force God's Hand to bring about our redemption through mercy and without delay.

Now, what line of action should we take to trigger Israel's redemption? The answer lies in a straightforward equation. Considering that it is God's natural propensity to grant compassion, kindness and love – it remains up to the Jewish individual to facilitate or to impede that Divine inclination. How so? Rabbi Akiva teaches that when the Jewish People fulfill God's wishes, they add strength to the heavenly spheres. They justify God's yearning to give.[8] Such is the message conveyed by King David: "*be'Elokim na'asei chayil*" – "we shall add strength to Hashem."[9] Through the observance of the Torah commandments, Israel reinforces God's readiness to bestow only blessings upon Am Yisrael. This extraordinary idea is equally suggested in Psalms 68:35: "*tenu oz le'Elokim*" – "give power to God." It is an unimaginable concept where man would assign might to the Creator. Nonetheless, through the observance of Shabbat and the *mitzvot*, we overrule the prosecuting arguments against Israel and we justify God's readiness to forgive and bless us with peace and prosperity.

Likewise, when Israel disregards God's commandments, they weaken, as it were, His natural eagerness to deliver unrestrained abundance. This exceptional concept is present in Moses's rebuke: "*Tsur yeladkha teshi*" – "you weakened the Rock Who gave birth to you."[10] How can Israel weaken God? It is by transgressing His commandments. In doing so, they also reinforce the forces of impurity across the world, thus prolonging the exile and causing wars and suffering. The Mishna further highlights this idea in urging: "*da' ma'lemala mimakh*" – You [the Jewish individual] ought to know that all decisions made in heaven are caused by your actions."[11] The fearful heavenly decrees as well as the favorable Divine decisions find their origin in the behavior of the Jewish individual."[12] Eventually, dear reader, Israel's redemption will originate "*mimakh*," from you. All the deliberations taking place in heaven concerning the destiny of mankind in general and of Am Yisrael in particular, are determined by you. The sanctity of Shabbat and the Jewish holidays, as highlighted in this book, along with the lasting wisdom of their message are conducive to achieving this beneficial awareness. Undeniably, despite the turbulent perils it faces, Israel's redemption is approaching slowly but surely. ■

8 *Eicha Rabati* 6:1 – *Nefesh HaChaim* 1:3

9 Psalms 60:14

10 Deuteronomy 32:18

11 *Avot* 2:1

12 *Likutim of Rav Issachar Dov Rubin zt"l* , *Nefesh HaChaim* 1:4

נר ה׳׳ נשמת אדם
In Memoriam, למנוחת ועילוי נשמת

to my dear parents
Shimon Haim ben Harav Eliyahu Gabay, *z"l*
He pursued righteousness and kindness
Soulika Gabay bat Harav Haim Halahmi, *z"l*
Humble and righteous, she led a life of prayers

Simi R'bibo bat Harav Eliyahu Gabay, *z"l*
Shlomo R'bibo ben Messoud, *z"l*

Marcelle Messody Castiel bat Mesoud, *z"l*

Shaul ben Simcha, *z"l*
Yitzhak ben Simcha, *z"l*
Shaul ben Rachel, *z"l*
Adela Chaya bat Mazal, *z"l*

Sina bat Esther, *z"l*
Gina Malka bat Esther, *z"l*
Eliyahu ben Mazal, *z"l*
Esther bat Gutcha, *z"l*
Yosef ben Miriam Freue, *z"l*
Mazal Fortune bat Sarah, *z"l*

Harav Avner Abensour ben Gabriel, *z"l*

Yeshayah Chaim ben Meir Hacohen, *z"l*
Chaya Rivkah bat Leibel Halevy, *z"l*
Zalman ben Yehezkel Dov, *z"l*

נר ה" נשמת אדם

In Memoriam, **למנוחת ועילוי נשמת**

Pinchas ben Mazal Krief, *z"l*

Harav Mordechai ben Daniel, *z"l*
Rachel bat Eliyahu Bayar, *z"l*
Shimon ben Pesach, *z"l*

Avraham ben Baruch Laureano, *z"l*

Akiva ben Yeshayahu, *z"l*
Rachel bat Arieh Leib, *z"l*

Mordechai ben Yosef Leibowitz, *z"l*
Devorah bat Nachum, *z"l*

Shimon ben Avraham, *z"l*
David ben Shmuel, *z"l*

Rina bat Rivkah Abekasis, *z"l*

Yaakov Eliahu ben Eliezer, *z"l*
Leah Aidel bat Moshe Arie, *z"l*
Chaim ben Yaakov Dov, *z"l*
Esther bat Mordechai, *z"l*

אלה יעמדו לברכה

These shall stand for the blessing

Moshe ben Rachamim
Ashraf bat Yosef
Sharona bat Hamda

Eliyahu Meir, Sarah, Shlomo Yisrael,
Simy Odelia, and Rivka Emanuelle R'bibo

Esther, Devorah and Aryeh Laureano

Dedicated by the Zaguy Family to
Moshe and his wife Nahid and to their children
Michael and MIchelle